THE JOURNAL JURISPRUDENCE

VOLUME SIX

"CONTEMPORARY LEGAL THEORY"

Contributors

Mr Thomas Kupka
University of Bremen

Mr Samuel Alexander
University of Melbourne

Mr Max McCann
New York City Law Department

Ms. Donna M. Lyons
New York University

Professor Bidzina Savaneli
University of Tbilisi

Guest Editor

Dr.Jur. Eric Engle
Harvard University

Editor

Mr Aron Ping D'Souza
University of Melbourne

TRINITY TERM
APRIL 2010

Elias Clark

PUBLISHED BY THE ELIAS CLARK GROUP

DISTRIBUTED IN CONNECTION WITH THE GALE GROUP,
A PART OF CENGAGE LEARNING

(2010) J. JURIS 107

The Elias Clark Group
www.elias-clark.com

GPO Box 5001
Melbourne, Victoria 3001
Australia

First Published 2010.

Cataloguing-in-Publication entry

Editor:	D'Souza, Aron Ping.
Authors:	D'Souza, Aron Ping. Engle, Eric. Kupka, Thomas. Alexander, Samuel. McCann, Max. Lyons, Donna M. Savaneli, Bidzina.
Title:	The Journal Jurisprudence, Volume Six, "Contemporary Legal Theory."
ISBN:	978-0-9807318-3-5 (pbk.)
ISSN:	1836-0955
Subjects:	Law – jurisprudence. Philosophy –general.

This edition may be cited as

(2010) J. Juris.

followed by the page number

ABOUT THE TYPEFACE

The Journal Jurisprudence is typeset in Garamond 12 and the footnotes are set in Garamond 10. The typeface was named for Claude Garamond (c. 1480 - 1561) and are based on the work of Jean Jannon. By 1540, Garamond became a popular choice in the books of the French imperial court, particularly under King Francis I. Garamond was said to be based on the handwriting of Angelo Vergecio, a librarian to the King. The italics of Garamond are credited to Robert Grandjon, an assistant to Claude Garamond. The font was re-popularised in the art deco era and became a mainstay on twentieth-century publication. In the 1970s, the font was redesigned by the International Typeface Corporation, which forms the basis of the variant of Garamond used in this Journal.

TABLE OF CONTENTS

<u>CALL FOR PAPERS</u>

The field of jurisprudence lies at the nexus of law and politics, the practical and the philosophical. By understanding the theoretical foundations of law, jurisprudence can inform us of the place of legal structures within larger philosophical frameworks. In its inaugural edition, *The Journal Jurisprudence* received many creative and telling answers to the question, "What is Law?" For the second edition, the editors challenged the scholarly and lay communities to inquire into intersection between jurisprudence and economics.

With the backing of our diverse and disparate community, *The Journal Jurisprudence* has now evolved into a more diverse form. We will no longer be setting a question for each issue, but instead designing issues around the articles we received. Therefore, we invite scholars, lawyers, judges, philosophers and lay people tackle the any and all of the great questions of law. Knowing that ideas come in all forms, papers can be of any length, although emphasis is placed on readability by lay audiences.

Papers may engage with case studies, philosophical arguments or any other method that answers philosophical question applicable to the law. Importantly, articles will be selected based upon quality and the readability of works by non-specialists. The intent of the Journal is to involve non-scholars in the important debates of legal philosophy.

The Journal also welcomes and encourages submissions of articles typically not found in law journals, including opinionated or personalised insights into the philosophy of law and its applications to practical situations.

Jurisprudence is published four times per year, to coincide with the four terms of the legal year, in an attractive paperback and electronic edition.

All authors who submit to this edition will be provided with a complementary copy of the journal.

Length: Any length is acceptable, although readability to non-specialist is key.

Presentation Style: Papers must comply with the Australian Guide to Legal Citations, Second Edition published by the Melbourne University Law Review. An electronic edition is available at, http://mulr.law.unimelb.edu.au/PDFs/aglc_dl.pdf

Submission: You must submit electronically in Microsoft Word format to editor@jurisprudence.com.au. Extraneous formatting is discouraged.

Correspondence can also be sent to this address. If you are considering submitting an article, you are invited to contact the editor to discuss ideas before authoring a work.

SUBSCRIPTION INFORMATION

The Journal is published four times per year in an attractive softcover book. Subscription to the Journal can be achieved by two methods:

1) Single issues can be purchased on amazon.com. Our publishers, the Elias Clark Group, set a retail price for each edition, typically AU$40. However, due to their agreement with amazon.com, the price may vary for retail customers.

2) A subscription to the Journal can be purchased for AU$150 per year, or AU$280 for two years. This price includes postage throughout the world. Payment can be made by international bank cheque, but not a personal cheque, to:

   The Journal Jurisprudence,
   C/o The Elias Clark Group
   GPO Box 5001
   Melbourne, Victoria, Australia.

Alternatively, the Journal is available online at www.jurisprudence.com.au and can be read there free of charge.

INTRODUCTION

Dr.Jur. Eric Engle, a brilliant theoretician and burgeoning leader of the field of legal philosophy, generously accepted an invitation to guest edit this edition.

As regular readers will know, Dr Engle is an ambidextrous scholar who has made many contributions to diverse areas of legal theory. In this spirit, he has curated five significant articles for this issue of *Jurisprudence*. He has brought together a diverse cornucopia of scholars who write articles of such quality that I have no doubt that they will be cited by scholars, practitioners and students for years to come.

The title of the edition, "Contemporary Legal Theory," reflects the advancing change in jurisprudence. No longer is jurisprudence a dichotomy between realism and positivism, but a field in flux. There is a cacophony of debates raging in the philosophy of law, which will emerge, I am sure, as a symphony of the theoretical. This issue, I hope, offers some insight into the current debates whilst encouraging resolution and inspiring further inquiry.

In the coming year, we have issues on negligence and jurisprudence, and on rationalisation in law. Both are shaping up to be blockbuster issues, with significant contributions in both.

Aron Ping D'Souza
Editor
Oxford, England
7 April 2010

EDITORIAL: CONTEMPORARY LEGAL THEORY

"Die Menschenwuerde ist unantastbar" – Human dignity is inviolable. So starts Article One of Germany's Basic Law (Grundgesetz). After the nightmare of mass murder and the disrespect of human rights, no calmer yet more radical statement of the central role of human rights in the Post-Westphalian era can be found. In this issue of the Journal, Jurisprudence we examine what Duncan Kennedy calls "post-positivist integration" – the rise of a constitutionalised and juridified global *legal* system centred on human rights, economic freedom, and seeking to attain peace through prosperity via the rule of law and open borders.

As your guest editor I am pleased to say we have found several exciting and thought provoking essays for your consideration each of which addresses one or more aspects of post-positivist integration.

First, Thomas Kupka in *Constitutional Nominalism* discusses the idea of legal formalism before the California Courts in the context of human rights - gay marriage. This article outlines the conflict between text and justice. The German tendency to clear terminological analysis of law shines through here: while we might disagree with the result of the California Court's decision, we are compelled to accept that, in mechanical terms, the Court's decision is correctly reasoned. More interestingly, Kupka points out the different results which obtained in the Court's decision when interpreting a *statute* as opposed to the opposite result when analyzing essentially the same text in the *constitution.* Again, doctrinal discipline and clarity mark the German approach to law, belying claims of radical legal indeterminacy.

Continuing with global perspectives, the second article, *Earth Jurisprudence* by Samuel Alexander seeks to develop a "Gaia" centric jurisprudence aimed not at irrational "growth" but rather at sustainable development. Alexander's piece can be seen as a "green" perspective as an alternative to "constant growth" of neoliberalism.

Max McCann gives us a longer third article, *The True Cost of Economic Rights Jurisprudence.* McCann examines the conflict between individual (i.e. fundamental…) human rights and economism at great length and in depth. He concludes the that the usual opposition of individual rights to economic rights is a false dichotomy. While I happen to think that fundamental rights are inalienable and thereby distinct from alienable economic rights, I also think that the level of attainment of human rights in materialist terms depends very much on economic development – that richer societies are better at securing basic human rights than poorer ones. While economic rights and individual rights are often interwoven – McCann's point – I must point out that fundamental rights are such precisely because they are of higher value to society than the economic factors on which they depend, i.e. there are axiological as well as ontological differences between fundamental rights and economic rights. Once more, the dialectical method helps us attain precision in understanding the interactions of fundamental human rights and economic rights. We look forward to seeing McCann deepen his ideas to meet those counterpoints.

Donna Lyons, a rising jurist, presents our fourth and most detailed article. She examines hermeneutic theory, and concludes it is essentially a doomed enterprise due to the inherent subjectivity of any theorist. While I think dialectical materialism allows us to find the closest approximation to truth, her warning to other theorists is well put. In her own words, "Theories purporting to provide universal truths about the nature of law are fallible and thus do not provide necessary truths because such theories must be founded on presuppositions which are reflections of fallible intuitions." For Lyons (I believe I agree) conceptual analysis is no escape, for it too is ultimately founded on intuitions - subjective presuppositions. Furthermore, "the tendency of the legal theorist to superimpose her own intuitions onto those of her subjects renders her results even more likely to be erroneous." I can only reiterate her argument which is complex, nuanced and cogent, yet analyses what, to me, is new ground. Her argument in sum is this:

"1) Hermeneutics is a method used by the theorist which involves understanding a social system from the perspective of the social subject.

2) A majority of legal philosophers use hermeneutics during theory-construction.

3) Using hermeneutics does not mean that a philosopher must endorse a specifically moral position but it does mean that reliance on personal intuitions is inevitable.

4) Legal positivists who employ hermeneutics cannot claim to have discovered the nature of law because reliance on intuitions, which is inevitable, produces faulty results.

5) Rather than making false claims regarding law's nature, we, as philosophers, ought to strive to accept law as an essentially contested concept, and thereby acknowledge the limitations that are placed on our pursuit by intuitionism, but remain satisfied to choose between theories of law based on their pragmatic value."

The overall argument is brilliant, even if points of it can be contested.

Inasmuch as hermeneutics is one more variety of discourse theory I agree with Lyons, that much of liberal legal theory is "a blind alley". However, I also think that through materialism we are able to ground theoretical claims which enables an objective dialectical synthesis – the closest possible approximation of truth, i.e. "best practice". Essentially, Lyons is arguing against philosophical dualism. We look forward to seeing her grapple with monism versus dualism as well as with dialectics and materialism in the construction of legal science in her future works. I am certain they will be at at least as brilliant as her critique of hermeneutics and we are certain to hear more from this young brilliant theorist.

As to dialectical materialism, Professor Bidzina Savaneli in our final article describes a dialectics between human rights in national and international law and between positivism and natural law in the second article. He argues, quite correctly, that human rights are now the focal point of the international system, the sine qua non of the juridified and constitutionalized international legal system. I share his point on the central character of human rights in the post-Westphalian international system – and so does Professor Duncan Kennedy. Interestingly, Professor Savaneli seems to argue that positive law states what ought to be and that moral theory, as a reflection of the material facts of society states what is – a reversal of the usual correspondence between positivism as "is" and moral theory as "ought". While I happen to think that the is/ought dichotomy arises from misreadings of Hume, and thus is a blind alley, the supposition that one cannot infer "ought" from "is" is so prevalent that Professor Savaneli's article is noteworthy at least in that context – as well as for raising the idea of dialectics in law. Moreover, he points us to interesting legal scholars from the Caucuses who might otherwise go unnoticed due to distance and language. Professor Savaneli also, to my view rightly, critiques Kelsen, and also argues that comparative legal theory should not merely compare laws within one system (civilianist or common law) but also between different systems. Professor Savaneli's post-positivist theory is interesting and highly relevant as an example of the post-positivist consolidation of legal theory currently taking place within contemporary legal thought. Whether this consolidation can lead to peaceful global governance via human rights is one of the key practical questions of our epoch. I believe it will be answered in the affirmative.

Post-positivist integration (i.e. consolidation of "Empire") is the current reality facing legal theory. Whether one supports or opposes globalism from the "left" or the "right" all of these articles manage to address key points in contemporary legal theory. Taken together I hope that they help the reader understand a key contradiction in contemporary legal thought:

1) Human rights are the centrepiece of the constitutionalized and juridified post-Westphalian international system.
2) Classical liberal theory cannot construct rights discourse effectively due to individualism, subjectivism, and discourse theory.
I believe these weaknesses in contemporary liberal theory which undermine globalizing constitutionalization and juridification of human rights can be surmounted using dialectics and materialism. Seen in this perspective, the articles presented hopefully take on deeper meaning due to greater context.

We wish to thank the authors heartily for their kind contributions. And, to our readers: *Bonne lecture!*

Dr.Jur. Eric Engle, Guest Editor, the Journal, Jurisprudence

NAMES AND DESIGNATIONS IN LAW: TOWARDS A NOMINALIST APPROACH TO CONSTITUTIONAL JURISPRUDENCE[1]

Thomas Kupka

I.

In a constitutional democracy, the people have the last word – or a Constitutional Court. And such a Court has to, inter alia, ensure that the people retain the power to give their word. Now, the people's vote often is difficult to predict and, on occasion, even contradictory. A Constitutional Court, in contrast, has to maintain the continuity of the Constitution, adjust it to the changing times but also ensure that the political conditions do not compromise its substance. The well-understood balance between continuity and change, therefore, belongs to the noblest tasks of constitutional jurisprudence. The California Supreme Court, however, has shown quite a remarkable turn in this respect: In May 2009 it confirmed in *Strauss v. Horton*[2], by a majority of 6:1, an amendment to the California Constitution, which now reads: "Only marriage between a man and a woman is valid or recognized in California"[3], whereas it declared a year before in *In re Marriage Cases,* a statutory family law provision[4] with exactly the same formulation, unconstitutional because retention of the traditional definition of marriage did not constitute a state interest sufficiently compelling, under the strict scrutiny equal protection standard, to justify withholding that status from same-sex couples.[5]

In both instances the reviewed provisions have come about by direct-democratic legislative initiatives. The fact that constitutional amendments can be adopted by initiative is a specialty of California law and is regarded as a particularly democratic feature of the California Constitution.[6] In the current

---

[1] Thanks to Chad Crowe for a help with the language and to Eric Engle for the editorial fine-tuning.

[2] KAREN L. STRAUSS, et al., Petitioners, v. MARK B. HORTON, et al. The decision is of May 26, 2009 and is published under: http://www.courtinfo.ca.gov/opinions/documents/S168047.PDF. Page numbers in this article refer to the pages there.

[3] Cal. Const., Art. I, § 7.5.

[4] California Family Code, § 308.5.

[5] *In re Marriage Cases*, 43 Cal. 4th 757 (May 2008).

[6] Cal. Const., Art. II, § 8, subd. (b); Art. XVIII, §§ 3 and 4. Seventeen more states, though, permit constitutional amendments to be proposed through the initiative process. These states are: Arizona (Ariz. Const., art. 4, pt. 1, § 1(2)), Arkansas (Ark. Const., art. 5, § 1), Colorado (Colo. Const., art. V, § 1(1)), Florida (Fla. Const., art. XI, § 3), Illinois (Ill. Const., art. XIV, § 3), Massachusetts (Mass. Const., amend. art. XLVIII, pt. II, § 2), Michigan (Mich. Const., art.

case, however, the people decided with 52% of the votes cast for the proposed amendment (the so-called *Proposition 8*) and thus against same-sex marriage. But while petitioners insisted with *In re Marriage* that homosexual couples, in addition to their right to register as domestic partners[7], also have the right to a civil marriage, the Court now holds that the new amendment means only a change in language, not in case – and is therefore only a case of different names.

This interpretation seems to allow for a legal concept which might be called Constitutional Nominalism. Thus, after a brief overview of the Court's reasoning (**II**), I shall try to assess the decision in light of some reflections on nominalist philosophy (**III**).

II.

The California Supreme Court's current ruling, and seemingly contradictory stance to the decision the year before, was generally surprising. Crucially, the new amendment immediately took effect the day after the election. Thus, says the Court in *Strauss v. Horton*, the Constitution is now a different one than in May 2008 when it decided *In re Marriage*. Accordingly, the opinion goes, while *In re Marriage* was concerned with a statutory provision limiting marriage to a union between a man and a woman under state constitutional provisions that did not expressly permit or prescribe such a limitation, the principal issue in *Strauss* concerned the scope of the right of the people, under the provisions of the California Constitution, to change or alter the state Constitution itself through the initiative process so as to incorporate such a limitation as an explicit section of it.[8]

XII, § 2), Mississippi (Miss. Const., art. 15, § 273), Missouri (Mo. Const., art. III, § 49), Montana (Mont. Const., art. XIV, § 9), Nebraska (Neb. Const., art. III, §§ 1, 2), Nevada (Nev. Const., art. 19, § 2), North Dakota (N.D. Const., art. III, §§ 1, 9), Ohio (Ohio Const., art. II, §§ 1, 1a), Oklahoma (Okla. Const., art. 5, §§ 1, 2), Oregon (Or. Const., art. IV, §§ 1, 2), and South Dakota (S.D. Const., art. XXIII, § 1).

7 California Family Code, §§ 297 ff.: "Domestic Partner Registration".

8 I leave aside a second strand of the decision which concerns the question whether Proposition 8 is a constitutional *revision* rather than an amendment. A *revision* to the California Constitution may be proposed either by two thirds of each house of the Legislature or by a constitutional convention; Cal. Const., Art. XVIII, §§ 1 and 2. For our purpose it suffices that, according to the court, "the *amendment* process *never* has been reserved only for minor or unimportant changes to the state Constitution"; *Strauss v. Horton*, ibid. 93 (original italics). In this respect the court points out that the right of women to vote in California, the initiative, referendum, and recall powers themselves, an explicit right of privacy, and even the reinstatement of the death penalty, all came about by constitutional amendment; ibid., 93 f.

Given the great importance of direct democracy in the California Constitution the Court felt hesitant to intervene. Justice Kennard, who also signed the majority opinion in *In re Marriage*, explains in her concurring opinion, how she sees the court's function in this respect: "My view on this issue has not changed. Interpreting and enforcing the state Constitution is a judicial responsibility, and the judiciary's duty to exercise this authority is particularly important and grave when constitutionally guaranteed rights and freedoms are at stake. What has changed, however, is the state Constitution that this Court interpreted and enforced in the *Marriage Cases*. [...] Although the people through the initiative power *may not change* this Court's interpretation of language in the state Constitution, they *may change* the constitutional language itself, and thereby enlarge or reduce the personal rights that the state Constitution as so amended will thereafter guarantee and protect. [...] Although this Court's decision in the *Marriage Cases* [...] remains the final word on the meaning of the state Constitution *as it then read*, the people have now used their initiative power to refashion the wording of the California Constitution and by this means have altered its substance, and thus its meaning, as of the effective date of the initiative measure".[9] In such a case it is the Court's duty to reconcile the new provision with the other constitutional norms.

What again was at stake was the constitutional right to marry, as embodied in the *privacy* and *due process clauses* of the California Constitution (art. I, §§ 1, 7), and the state's *equal protection guarantee* (art. I, § 7). And here, the Court already observed in *In re Marriage* that "in recent decades, there has been a fundamental and dramatic transformation in this state's understanding and legal treatment of gay individuals and gay couples" resulting in a general recognition "that gay individuals are entitled to the same legal rights and the same respect and dignity afforded all other individuals and are protected from discrimination on the basis of their sexual orientation".[10] Thus, the Court concluded, "that the right to marry, as embodied in article I, sections 1 and 7 of the California Constitution, guarantees same-sex couples the same substantive constitutional rights as opposite-sex couples to choose one's life partner and enter with that person into a committed, officially recognized, and protected family relationship that enjoys all of the constitutionally based incidents of marriage".[11]

---

[9] *Strauss v. Horton*, Kennard, J., concurring, S. 2 f. (original italics).
[10] *In re Marriage*, ibid. 821-822
[11] Ibid., 829

In *Strauss v. Horton*, the Court contends, this has not changed. It is merely the constitutional language which would be different now. And in light of *In re Marriage*, the majority opinion emphasizes, "[p]roposition 8 reasonably must be interpreted in a limited fashion as eliminating only the right of same-sex couples to equal access to the *designation* of marriage, and as not otherwise affecting the constitutional right of those couples to establish an officially recognized family relationship".[12] The term "marriage" is reserved for heterosexual couples and the corresponding determination in the constitutional text via constitutional amendment is reserved for the people.

III.

Is same-sex civil union only a matter of name and designation? As I said, one could take this for some kind of Constitutional Nominalism. Nominalism suffers from a bad reputation and has (perhaps wrongly) been attributed to the English philosopher William of Ockham who turned from the Aristotelian categories to experience and semantics.[13] Three centuries later, Thomas Hobbes opposed the empirical aspect of law to the natural law tradition and noted law's ability to be modified arbitrarily. For him, language is not just a tool for mapping the world, it also changes the world. Language alone, as Hobbes already knew, is capable of constituting human reality, particularly political reality. But as such, language remains artificial. And it is this, which makes things replaceable by names and designations and linkable in new ways, freeing them from their merely natural causal relations and making them objects of the will of the itself artificial person.[14]

Nominalism, in Hobbes as well as in Ockham, started with the rejection of universals. In a more modern sense, it implies the rejection of abstract objects, objects that are neither spatial nor temporal, and which, though not already in

---

12 *Strauss v. Horton*, ibid., 37 (italics added); see also ibid., 7 f., 11, 36 ff., 42 f., 92 f.

13 See e.g. Ph. Boehner, The Realistic Conceptualism of William Ockham, in: *Traditio* 4 (1946), 307 ff. In his article "William of Ockham" for the *Stanford Encyclopedia of Philosophy* (Edward N. Zalta, ed.) Paul Vincent Spade notes: "[Ockham's] originality and influence should not be exaggerated. For all his deserved reputation, his logical views are sometimes completely derivative and occasionally very idiosyncratic"; -- citations omitted. For new literature on Ockham see especially C. Panaccio, *Les mots, les concepts et les choses. Le sémantique de Guillaume d'Occam et le nominalisme d'aujourd'hui*, 1991.

14 Th. Hobbes, *Leviathan*, esp. chs. 4 and 5. See also Hobbes, *Elements of Philosophy. De corpore*, Part I, chs. 2-6, in: The English Works of Thomas Hobbes (Molesworth ed.), vol. I, 1839; and *Elements of Law*, Part I, chs. 1-5, ebd. vol. IV, 1840, See also C. Leijenhorst, Sense and Nonsense About Sense: Hobbes and the Aristotelians on Sense Perception and Imagination, in: P. Springboorg (ed.), *The Cambridge Companion to Hobbes's Leviathan*, 2007, 82 ff.

Aristotle, but at least since Kant's Table of Categories[15], are supposed to belong to the conditions of possibility of our knowledge and experience. As John Stuart Mill once famously summarized, early nominalism put it this way: "there is nothing general except names".[16] In our time, the notion that philosophy should abstain from classical ontology owes much to the writings of Nelson Goodman[17] who, along with Wilfrid Sellars[18], John Searle[19], and others, paved the road to what today is called Constructivism in science. Conversely, much of this constructivism, as Ian Hacking has observed, is motivated by an often unstated nominalist view.[20] Both sides, however, are dubious about the idea that reality has an intrinsic structure that science accurately describes. These doubts are raised by the notorious, persistent, seemingly insoluble perplexities to which the notion of "intrinsic" gives rise. The most familiar of these is the question: How can we ever hope to compare reality as it is in itself, naked and undescribed, with our descriptions of it? Many philosophers rebuked the notions of "intrinsic" and "in itself", as a result of the failure to answer that question. Instead, they look on the language we use to describe, and foremost *name*, the world and the problems we have with it. And again, it was Hobbes who already spoke against "those insignificant words, *abstract substance, separated essence*, and the like", and against "that confusion of words derived from the Latin verb *est*".[21]

But most importantly, the nominalist dissolution of classical metaphysics and, with it, the rejection of the possibility of a priori knowledge, makes language appear in historical perspective. Indeed, when the world no longer can be judged by the "nature of things", but instead belongs to man's eponymous sovereignty, then any language, along with its history of denotation, grammar, and syntax can be understood as a variation of a logic of historical experience.[22]

---

[15] In his *Critique of Pure Reason*, Kant arrives at his list of categories by first enumerating the forms of possible judgment (B95/A70-B109/A93).

[16] J. S. Mill, *System of Logic*, Book I, ch. 5, § 3 (citing Hobbes), in: Collected Works (J. M. Robson, ed.), vol. VII, 1963 ff.

[17] N. Goodman, *The Structure of Appearance*, 1951/3rd ed., 1977; see also his *Ways of Worldmaking*, 1978.

[18] See esp. W. Sellars, Empiricism and the Philosophy of Mind, in his *Science, Perception and Reality*, 1963. See also J. Seibt, *Properties as Processes, A Synoptic Study of Wilfrid Sellars' Nominalism*, 1990.

[19] J. Searle, *Speech Acts*, 1969; see also Searle, *The Construction of Social Reality*, 1995.

[20] I. Hacking, *The Social Construction of What?*, 1999, 80-84. And see esp. ibid., 83 f., Footnote 14, where Hacking's own use of the concept of "nominalism", interestingly, comes close to Kant's transcendental idealism.

[21] *De corpore*, ibid, ch. 3, No. 4 (original italics).

[22] See also H.-G. Gadamer, *Wahrheit und Methode*, Gesammelte Werke Bd. 1, 1990, 439 f.; engl. trans. *Truth and Method*, 2nd rev. edition, 1989, part III, ch. 2 (c).

In one form or another, this idea runs through the thoughts of authors as diverse as Nietzsche or Wittgenstein, Habermas or Derrida, as well as from W. v. O. Quine and Donald Davidson to Richard Rorty.[23] The often pejorative use of the word nominalism, along with its accusation of arbitrariness – usually, that linguistic arbitrariness causes arbitrariness in things – is therefore neither warranted in terms of language nor in terms of substance. Rather, it is necessary, as the Rolling Stones would have it, to "shine a light" on *understanding*[24], which in our context is the understanding of language. And what is true for philosophical hermeneutics applies to legal hermeneutics as well.

Jeremy Bentham was perhaps the first who took this route. He developed a radically empiricist theory of the meaning of words, which supported his utilitarianism and legal positivism.[25] Later, H.L.A. Hart, following Bentham's path, used the new developments in the philosophy of language to 'elucidate' the concept of law. He did so in studying the work of Ludwig Wittgenstein, and also the Oxford 'ordinary language' philosophers such as J. L. Austin. Hart suggested a basic "rule of recognition" that allows for the identification of law and which, as such, is a matter of (linguistic) convention.[26] Hence, this rule is not made valid by another legal rule; it is a "social rule". Hart claimed that such a social rule is a regular pattern of conduct accompanied by a "distinctive normative attitude", which "consists in the standing disposition of individuals to take such patterns of conduct both as guides to their own future conduct and as standards of criticism".[27] Basically, though, Hart described the rule of recognition circularly: From the social acceptance of the rule and its manifesting in legal practice he inferred the rule to exist, and then used its existence to identify the law.

Subsequently, other legal philosophers have dismissed the view that linguistic conventions can explain the rule of law. Ronald Dworkin, as one of the leading authors, has opposed Hart's theory on the basis that his whole approach to

---

23 I don't, of course, want to insinuate that all of the mentioned authors are "nominalists". All of them, however, think that truth is a property of sentences which again are dependent upon the vocabularies they consist of. Most pointedly this was elaborated by Richard Rorty, *Contingency, Irony, and Solidarity*, 1989, esp. ch. 1. And, for the last time now, already by Hobbes: "[F]or truth consists in speech, and not in the things spoken of"; *De corpore*, ibid., ch. 3, No. 7.

24 Besides H.-G. Gadamer, *supra*, see G. H. von Wright, *Explanation and Understanding*, 1971.

25 See J. Bentham, *Of Laws in General* (H.L.A Hart ed.) 1970; see also G.J. Postema, *Bentham and the Common Law Tradition*, 1986.

26 "[…] the rule of recognition exists only as a complex, but normally concordant, practice of the courts, officials, and private persons in identifying the law by reference to certain criteria. Its existence is a matter of fact"; H.L.A. Hart, *The Concept of Law*, 1961, 107 (2nd ed. 1994).

27 Ibid., 255

legal philosophy is undermined or "stung" by his approach to words – that Hart wrongly thought that lawyers all follow certain linguistic criteria for judging legal propositions.[28] Dworkin's so called "semantic sting" argument has set an agenda for much recent debate in the philosophy of law.[29] It implies that there must be more to the concept of legal validity than can be explained by a set of shared criteria embodied in a basic rule of recognition. This touches on the question about the relation between fact and value in law, and between law and morality. This question, according to Dworkin, can only be answered by what he famously called "Law as Integrity", a method of interpretation which owes much to John Rawls' "Justice as Fairness" and takes the moral underpinnings of law into account.[30] And, what has been most controversially discussed since: Dworkin claims that there is always a right answer to virtually every legal dispute – literally a Herculean task, especially for a court.[31]

We cannot determine the merits of this argument here in detail or whether such a Herculean judge, "[w]hen he intervenes in the process of government to declare some statute or other act of government unconstitutional, he does this in service of his most conscientious judgement about what democracy really is and what the Constitution, parent and guardian of democracy, really means".[32] What we can determine, however, is that whatever such a judge is doing, he does it with words. This even more so as no constitutional text can be separated from the language of the society it governs. And to ensure that both stay in line over time is the foremost task of constitutional jurisprudence. This does not mean that interpretative reason necessarily resigns itself to historical tradition. Instead, we should view the circularity of the hermeneutic deployment of meaning as an opportunity to appropriately work through the changing meanings in society.[33] Or, as Martin Heidegger put it: "What is decisive is not to get out of the circle but to come into it the right way".[34] Constitutional jurisprudence, therefore, primarily is concerned with words, i.e. with names and designations. They define the things at stake.

Now, a particular sexual preference is certainly not something the state has to judge. Nevertheless, a democratic legislature must be able to decide what it considers a marriage. Whether this needs to be done in the constitution, one

---

[28] R. Dworkin, *Law's Empire*, 1986, 31 ff., 45 f.

[29] See, for instance, the essays in J. Coleman (ed.), *Hart's Postscript*, 2001.

[30] R. Dworkin, *Law's Empire*, 1986, chs. 6 and 7.

[31] R. Dworkin, *Law's Empire*, ibid., 239; see also his *A Matter of Principle*, 1985, esp. ch. 5.

[32] R. Dworkin, *Law's Empire*, ibid., 399.

[33] See e.g. D. C. Hoy, The Critical Circle: Literature, History, and Philosophical Hermeneutics, 1978.

[34] M. Heidegger, *Being and Time* (Macquarrie/Robinson trans.), 1962, 195 (§ 32).

can surely find questionable, and equally, that amending the constitution in California is so easy.[35] However, the California Supreme Court explicitly interpreted the new amendment in such a restricted way that it would not infringe the constitutionally protected right to choose one's life partner regardless of sexual orientation. It thereby, like the US-Supreme Court[36], unequivocally rejected the natural law tradition.[37] Rightly, the Court confronts the so called "inalienable" or natural personal rights with the same "inalienable" rights of the Californian people to amend the Constitution.[38] That in fact leads nowhere. And all the more so, as one certainly could ask whether a natural law argument would weaken rather than strengthen the case for same-sex marriage.

Against this background, the nominalism of the California Supreme Court is not so flawed. And it used an original hermeneutic standard when it related the new amendment to the other constitutional norms: "[W]hen constitutional provisions can reasonably be construed so as to avoid conflict, such a construction should be adopted. [...] As a means of avoiding conflict, a recent, specific provision is deemed to carve out an exception to and thereby limit an older, general provision".[39] Applied to the conflict of the present constitutional amendment with the fundamental interest of same-sex couples in having their family relationship accorded the same respect and dignity enjoyed by opposite-sex couples, the Court concluded: "[T]he measure carves out a narrow and limited exception to these state constitutional rights, reserving the official *designation* of the term "marriage" for the union of opposite-sex couples as a matter of state constitutional law, but leaving undisturbed all of the other extremely significant substantive aspects of a same-sex couple's state constitutional right to establish an officially recognized and protected family relationship and the guarantee of equal protection of the laws".[40]

Thus, this decision certainly cannot be accused of arbitrariness. Rather it can be seen as a well-balanced interpretive approach to the constitutional text, which takes into account both the customary language of the protected constitutional rights and the current, albeit traditional civic use of the term marriage. The result may disappoint some. It should not be underestimated, however, that the Court did not elevate itself to something like a language creator, but followed judicial restraint by merely setting the new amendment bindingly under the

[35] But this, as *Strauss v. Horton* makes clear, is not for the Court to determine; ibid., 12 f.

[36] See L. Tribe, *American Constitutional Law*, 3rd ed., 2000, 1335-1362.

[37] *Strauss v. Horton*, ibid., 11 f., 122 ff., 126,

[38] *Strauss v. Horton*, ibid., 124 ff.

[39] *Bowens v. Superior Court*, 1 Cal. 4th 36, 45 (1991).

[40] *Strauss v. Horton*, ibid., 7 (original emphasis); see also 35 ff.

other constitutional guarantees. In a Constitutional Democracy, creators of language, and legal language in particular, are the people who, if they find it necessary, also can use their power to amend the constitution in this respect. If one likes, it is only the "forceless force of the better argument" (Habermas) that counts here. But, so far as we can see, there is no guarantee for accuracy, or truth, external to language.

And since Thomas Kuhn has called attention to the contingent and contextual nature of our knowledge,[41] the overestimated belief in strict methodological criteria has lost its magical power too. The question, then, how we think and talk about things and what we make out of them in terms of them being "wrongly" or "rightly" perceived comes down to a matter of *fit*. This was basically the same in Kant.[42] Of course, we believe a proposition is true only if it fits our standards and criteria but, conversely, we hold our standards and criteria as true if they fit what we believe is right. It may suffice, then, if our reasoning leads to something like a "reflective equilibrium", which John Rawls once suggested.[43] The California Supreme Court in *Strauss v. Horton* reached such equilibrium within its authority.

One problem, though, remains. What happens to the estimated 18,000 same-sex marriages that were performed in California before the new amendment took effect? It is an old Common Law tradition that laws under *due process*-protection do not apply retroactively unless the legislature explicitly intends so. We don't need to go into detail here. It is enough to note that the California Supreme Court couldn't find such intention and thus concluded that *Proposition 8* should be interpreted to only apply prospectively and not to invalidate retroactively the marriages of same-sex couples performed prior to its effective date.[44] This, however, causes the implausible situation that there are now married same-sex couples within a state legal framework that reserves the term marriage exclusively for heterosexuals. So perhaps the California Supreme Court already should have deferred to the direct-democratic electorate in *In re Marriage*. It not only would have avoided the current problems, but also have kept the Constitution out of the maelstrom of everyday politics. The campaigns for a renewed constitutional amendment have already begun.[45]

41 Th. Kuhn, The Structure of Scientific Revolutions, 1962/1969.

42 See H. Putnam, *Reason, Truth, and History*, 1981, 60 ff., see also ibid., 123 (citing Nelson Goodman) and 133 f. (with reference to some sort of Aristotelian Eudaemonia).

43 J. Rawls, *A Theory of Justice*, 1971, 20 f, 48-51, and 120 f., following Nelson Goodman, *Fact, Fiction, Forecast*, 1955, 65-68, concerning the methods of deductive and inductive inference.

44 *Strauss v. Horton*, ibid., 128 ff.

45 *San Francisco Chronicle*: "Prop. 8 Stands; More Ballot Battles Ahead", of May 27, 2009, A 1.

California's Governor Arnold Schwarzenegger called the outcome of the initiative "unfortunate". Meanwhile, the California Supreme Court had spoken, and thus gave the last word back to the people. The democratic contest of opinions is the heart of a vibrant liberal society. And in this contest, as the Court expressly pointed out, the homosexual community can continue to seek a majority.[46] With only 52 to 48% of the votes for the new amendment they are very close.

46 *Strauss v. Horton*, ibid., 135: "Having determined that none of the constitutional challenges to the adoption of Proposition 8 have merit, we observe that if there is to be a change to the state constitutional rule embodied in that measure, it must "find its expression at the ballot box""; citing *In re Marriage Cases*, 43 Cal.4th 757, 884 (conc. & dis. opn. Corrigan, J.).

EARTH JURISPRUDENCE AND THE ECOLOGICAL CASE FOR DEGROWTH

Samuel Alexander*

If we do not change direction, we are likely to end up where we are going. – Chinese Proverb

Earth Jurisprudence seeks to redefine the relationship between human beings and the environment by abandoning the anthropocentrism of much contemporary legal theory in favour of an eco-centric perspective.[1] This shift in consciousness is seen as necessary because existing legal systems, by generally treating nature as a 'resource' to be exploited for human gratification, have failed to maintain the health and integrity of the ecosystems upon which the entire community of life depends.[2] What is urgently needed, and what Earth Jurisprudence promises, is a deep ecology of law, one normatively grounded on the idea that human law ought to reflect and respect the bio-physical laws of nature.

This paper explores the Earth Jurisprudence of economic growth, an area that has received almost no attention in this new body of literature[3] but one in which the themes and insights of Earth Jurisprudence are highly relevant. I will begin by describing the 'growth model of progress' which is implicit to most

* Samuel Alexander has been a lecturer at Melbourne Law School and is currently completing his PhD there. Contact: samuelalexander42@gmail.com.

1 Some leading texts in the small but provocative literature of Earth Jurisprudence include Cormac Cullinan, *Wild Law: A Manifesto for Earth Justice* (2002); Thomas Berry, *The Great Work* (1999) and *Evening Thoughts* (2006); Vandana Shiva, *Earth Democracy: Justice, Sustainability, and Peace* (2005); Christopher Stone, *Should Trees Have Standing? And Other Essays on Law, Morals, and the Environment* (1996); and Roderick Nash, *The Rights of Nature* (1986). For influential precursors, see Henry David Thoreau, *Walden* (1854); Aldo Leopold, *A Sand County Almanac* (1966); and Bill Devall and George Sessions, *Deep Ecology* (1985).

2 In 2005 the United Nations published a report, compiled and reviewed by over 2,000 leading scientists from ninety-five countries, which revealed that 60% of global ecosystem services are 'being degraded or used unsustainably,' resulting in 'substantial and largely irreversible loss in the diversity of life on Earth.' Millennium Ecosystem Assessment, *Ecosystems and Human Wellbeing: Synthesis* (2005) 1 <http://www.millenniumassessment.org/documents/document.356.aspx.pdf> at 20 June 2009. A number of similar studies are listed and briefly reviewed below.

3 The only study I have found is Joseph H. Guth, 'Cumulative Impacts: Death-Knell for Cost-Benefit Analysis in Environmental Analysis (2008) 11 *Barry Law Review* 23 (arguing that the law must abandon its use of cost-benefit economic analysis to justify individual environmental impacts and instead adopt the goal of maintaining the ecological integrity of the biosphere).

modern political ideologies, whether on the Left or the Right, and which we will see shares certain assumptions with law-and-economics scholarship. Put simply, the growth model assumes that the overall well-being of a society is approximately proportional to the size of its economy, in terms of Gross Domestic Product (GDP) per capita, since more money means that more social and individual 'preferences' can be satisfied via market transactions. From this perspective the answer to almost every problem – including environmental problems – is *more economic growth*. The notion of a macroeconomic 'optimal scale' is all but unthinkable. A bigger economy is simply better.

I wish to unpack the ecological consequences that flow from the growth model and argue that Earth Jurisprudence, by situating itself outside the growth model, has a very important role to play in the critique of growth and in the provision of an alternative conceptualization of 'nature' in law, especially property law where human-centred, economic analysis dominates. I base my analysis on the notion of 'degrowth,' an emerging term that designates a radical critique of economic growth. My basic argument is that when an economy has grown so large that it exceeds the regenerative and absorptive capacities of Earth's ecosystems, then lawmakers ought to initiate a 'degrowth' process of planned economic contraction. Only by doing so, I will conclude, can over-consuming societies begin repaying their ecological debts to the Wild.

The substantive part of the paper begins, as I have said, by outlining the growth model of progress. This dominant model propagates the pernicious myth of an infinitely expanding economy on a finite planet, a myth Earth Jurisprudence serves to undermine. I then cursorily review the credible body of environmental research which shows that the expanding global economy is ecologically unsustainable. Laying the foundations for an Earth Jurisprudence of economic growth, I then offer a brief history of 'growth scepticism,' the view that eventually an economy will reach an 'optimal scale' beyond which it should not grow. Since the scientific consensus firmly indicates that the 'optimal scale' has already been surpassed, I conclude that lawmakers in over-consuming societies ought to initiate a 'degrowth' process of planned economic contraction. I discuss this possibility in the context of property theory, speculating about what might become of the property systems of advanced capitalism should economic growth lose its privileged position as the touchstone of policy and institutional success. I close the paper with a fleeting discussion of 'the Wild,' in the hope of highlighting the ways in which the 'Transcendental' value of nature simply cannot be captured by the anthropocentric equations of economic analysis.[4]

---

[4] On 'the Wild,' see Jane Bennett, *Thoreau's Nature: Ethics, Politics, and the Wild* (2002).

Property, Wealth Maximization, and the Growth Model of Progress

Daniel Bell once noted that 'Economic growth is the secular religion of advancing industrial nations,'[5] suggesting that those nations have developed an unconditional faith in the God of Growth and are now prepared to sacrifice everything in its name. More recently, Clive Hamilton has observed:

> Nothing more preoccupies the modern political process than economic growth. As never before, it is the touchstone of policy success… [Political] parties may differ on social policy, but there is an unchallengeable consensus that the overriding objective of government must be growth of the economy.[6]

The defining assumption of our age, in other words, is that despite Western affluence much more economic growth is still needed to improve our lives. It is thought that more growth – and only more growth – can eliminate poverty, reduce inequality and unemployment, and properly fund schools, hospitals, the arts, scientific research, environmental protection programs, etc. Our great social problem, according to this popular narrative, is that even the richest nations do not have enough money to live well. And thus economic growth is heralded across much of the political spectrum as the goal towards which we must direct our collective energy.[7]

According to this 'growth model of progress,' the overriding objective of the property system is to facilitate economic growth as efficiently as possible, [8] a goal which is widely assumed to be best achieved when property rights are traded in 'free markets.' In the context of legal theory, 'free markets' have

---

5 Daniel Bell, *The Cultural Contradictions of Capitalism* (1976) 237.

6 Clive Hamilton, *Growth Fetish* (2003) 1-2.

7 Consider the Australian context, for example. In June 2004, in his 'Getting Things Right' speech, then Prime Minister John Howard stated: 'Maintaining a strong dynamic and growing economy is the… overriding responsibility of government.' Similarly, he elsewhere stated, 'The overriding aim of our agenda is to deliver Australia an annual economic growth rate of over four per cent on average during the decade to 2010.' Former labor Prime Minister Paul Keating said that if you could not grow the economy at over four percent a year, 'you might as well give the game away.' Cited in Richard Eckersley, 'The Challenge of Post-materialism' (March, 2005) *Australian Financial Review* 5-10.

8 For a recent, highly nuanced, expression of growth fetishism, see Benjamin M. Freidman, *The Moral Consequences of Economic Growth* (2005).

received their most systematic (and extreme) defence in the scholarship of law-and-economics, epitomized by the work of Richard Posner.[9] Making a representative statement on the economic analysis of property rights and market exchange, Posner writes:

> If every valuable (meaning scarce as well as desired) resource were owned by someone (universality), ownership connoted the unqualified power to exclude everybody else from using the resource (exclusivity) as well as to use it oneself, and ownership rights were freely transferable or as lawyers say alienable (transferable), value would be maximized.[10]

Leaving to one side the dubious assumptions about ownership, notice that 'value maximization' (or 'wealth maximization,' to use Posner's better known phrase) is held out as the proper function of the property system. Posner explains that wealth maximization is achieved when goods and other resources are in the hands of those who value them most, and someone values a good more only if he or she is both willing and able to pay more in money to have it.[11] The most efficient path to wealth maximization is through 'free markets,' Posner argues, in which private property is 'universal,' ownership is 'unqualified,' and ownership rights are 'freely transferable.'[12]

It should be noted at once that 'wealth maximization,' as the phrase is used in law-and-economics, and 'maximizing GDP' are not equivalent. Posner, in fact, has expressly distinguished them in his work, noting that 'wealth cannot be equated to GDP or any other *actual* pecuniary measure of value.'[13] Nevertheless, by looking to 'willingness to pay' (measured by actual pecuniary exchange) as the indicator of how various things are 'valued' in the marketplace,[14] Posner

---

9 See generally, Richard Posner, *Economic Analysis of Law* (3rd ed, 1986).

10 Ibid 32.

11 See Richard Posner, 'Utilitarianism, Economics, and Legal Theory' (1979) 8(1) *J Legal Studies* 103 and 'Wealth Maximization Revisited' (1985) 2 *Notre Dame L J* 85 (arguing that 'wealth maximization' provides an ethically attractive norm for social and political choices). See also, Richard Epstein, 'Why Restrain Alienation?' (1985) 85 *Colum. L Rev* 970 (arguing that no deviations from free-market alienability are permitted unless they are required by 'efficiency').

12 See Posner, above n 10.

13 See Posner, "Utilitarianism, Economics, and Legal Theory," above n 11, at 120 (emphasis in original).

14 On 'willingness to pay,' see Posner, 'Wealth Maximization Revisited,' above n 11, at 86.

ends up judging 'the Good' and 'the Right' in terms of dollars,[15] which is what the 'growth model' does by assuming economic growth is the best measure of 'progress.' Accordingly, although it would be a confusion to conflate 'wealth maximization' and the 'growth model of progress,' it is fair to say that the latter is based upon many of the assumptions of the former, meaning that there is some overlap in criticism.[16]

Since human beings are narrowly conceived of as self-interested, rational, independent consumers whose individual 'preferences' can be better satisfied with ever-more money,[17] the economic analysis of property aims to grow the economic pie as big as possible.[18] From this view, where *efficiency* is the governing ethical norm,[19] more economic pie is always better; and efficiency is defined as 'exploiting resources in such a way that "value" – human satisfaction as measured by aggregate willingness to pay for goods and services – is

[15] See, for example, Richard Posner, *Economics of Justice* (1981); and Guido Calabresi and Philip Bobbitt, *Tragic Choices* (1978). Some have argued that the normative theory beneath law-and-economics goes beyond simply being a narration of the political Right in the legal sphere and is also an attempt to resolve (by dressing economics up as a science) the ongoing difficulty of the relationship between law and politics. See Morton J Horowitz, "Law and Economics: Science or Politics," *Hofstra L R* 8 (1980): 905 and Mark Kelman, *A Guide to Critical Legal Studies* (1987) 114-185.

[16] The complex relationship between law-and-economics and the 'growth model' deserves closer analysis, however that task, a work in itself, must be put aside for another occasion. Despite criticizing several key assumptions of law-and-economics, I wish to clarify that the thesis of this paper is directed primarily at the 'growth model.' For an early but important critique of Posner's view, however, see Ronald Dworkin, "Is Wealth a Value?," *Journal of Legal Studies* 9 (1980): 191 and "Why Efficiency?," *Hofstra L R* 8 (1980): 563 (arguing that the normative failures of Posner's theory are so great that they cast doubt on its descriptive claims).

[17] For one formulation of this 'economic' conception of human beings, see Richard Posner, 'The Economic Approach to Law' (1975) 53 *Tex. L R* 757, 761, where he states: 'The basis of an economic approach to law is the assumption that the people involved with the legal system act as rational maximizers of their satisfactions.'

[18] Discussing the 'pie' metaphor, see Lucian A. Bebchuk, 'The Pursuit of a Bigger Pie: Can Everyone Expect a Bigger Slice' (1980) 8 *Hofstra L R* 671.

[19] Richard Posner, 'The Ethical and Political Basis of the Efficiency Norm in Common Law Adjudication' (1980) 8 *Hofstra L Rev* 487. Ronald Dworkin, Mark Kelman, and Duncan Kennedy, among many others, have leveled deep criticisms against attempts to construct the notion of 'efficiency' within the theory of law-and-economics as an ethical norm. A principal criticism is that 'wealth maximization' favors the advantaged for no justifiable reason. See, for example, Dworkin, above n 16; Jules L Coleman, 'Efficiency, Utility, and Wealth Maximization' (1980) 8 *Hofstra L R* 509; Duncan Kennedy and Frank Michelman, 'Are Property and Contract Efficient?' (1980) 8 *Hofstra L R* 711; Horowitz, above n 15; Lewis A Kornhauser, 'A Guide to the Perplexed Claims of Efficiency in the Law' (1980) 8 *Hofstra L R* 913; Kelman, above n 15; and Annalise Acorn, 'Valuing Virtue: Morality and Productivity in Posner's Theory of Wealth Maximization' (1994) 28 *Val U L R* 167.

maximized.'[20] The anthropocentrism here is stark and unabashed. Furthermore, the question of *sufficiency* – of how much economic pie is *enough* – does not arise.

This neoclassical perspective accepts that there is an 'optimal scale' at the *micro*economic level – which is to say, it accepts there will eventually come a point where growth in a *firm's* production will cost more than it is worth (and therefore be judged 'uneconomic' growth).[21] However, there is no place in neoclassicism for an 'optimal scale' at the *macro*economic level, no 'optimal scale' of the economy as a whole. This is because technological and allocative efficiency are thought to allow for an infinitely expanding economy, despite the obvious fact that we have but a single, finite planet to 'exploit.' Technological efficiency, it is assumed, will continually allow human beings to consume a finite set of resources more efficiently or, better yet, to consume a set of resources hitherto inaccessible. Allocative efficiency, it is assumed, will ensure that market mechanisms continually move resources into the hands of those who will 'exploit' them best. Upon these assumptions, the growth model purports to show that an economy can and should continue growing indefinitely. Economic growth, one is lead to believe, is always and everywhere the most direct path to increased human well-being.

Let us now consider how the neoclassical/neoliberal growth project has impacted on the life-support system we call Earth. By doing so the need for alternative perspectives on economic growth becomes obvious.

Unsustainable Growth and the Consumption of Natural Capital

There is now an overwhelming consensus within the scientific community that the high levels of economic growth and consumption in affluent societies today are environmentally unsustainable and certainly not universalizable.[22] Bill

---

20 Posner, above n 9, 10.

21 The term 'uneconomic' is often attributed to Herman Daly, whose work is discussed below. See Herman Daly, 'Uneconomic Growth in Theory and Fact' (1999) The First Annual Feasta Lecture, <www.feasta.org/documents/feastareview/daly.htm> at 20 May 2009. See also, Ezra Mishan, *The Costs of Economic Growth* (1967), also discussed below.

22 Exemplifying this consensus in 2005 was the panel of over 2,000 leading scientists assembled by the United Nations which issued a 'Millennium Ecosystem Assessment' report, finding that 'human actions are depleting the Earth's natural capital, putting such strain on the environment that the ability to sustain future generations can no longer be taken for granted.' See above n 2. Also, see the Union of Concerned Scientists (UCS), a science-based nonprofit affiliation of scientists/citizens with over 250,000 members. UCS publications include "World

McKibben even believes that the 'consensus' which has solidified over recent decades has transmogrified, in the last 18 months, into a 'panic,'[23] largely out of fear of approaching the ecological 'tipping point' beyond which feedback loops will be irreversible and unstoppable.[24] But even leaving to one side the dreadful possibility of a 'tipping point,' the best available evidence plainly illustrates that the global economy has physically grown to such a size that it now exceeds the regenerative and absorptive capacities of Earth's ecosystems.[25] That is, we are now consuming natural capital and diminishing the capacity of the planet to support life in the future.

A few recent studies will serve to reveal the depth and extent of this ecological crisis. Mathis Wackernagel and his colleagues have measured the 'ecological footprint' of humanity and compared it to the 'carrying capacity' of the planet.[26] They conclude that the global ecological footprint exceeds carrying capacity by approximately twenty percent. In 2006, *Redefining Progress*, a leading public policy think tank, reviewed and updated this claim and the methods used, concluding that the ecological footprint is now exceeding carrying capacity by nearly forty

Scientists' Warning to Humanity," issued in 1992 by 1,600 of the world's leading scientists, including the majority of Nobel laureates in the sciences, which begins: 'Human beings and the natural world are on a collision course. Human activities inflict harsh and often irreversible damage on the environment and on critical resources. If not checked, many of our current practices put at serious risk the future that we wish for human society and the plant and animal kingdoms, and may so alter the living world that it will be unable to sustain life in the manner that we know. Fundamental changes are urgent if we are to avoid the collision our present course will bring.' Towards the end of this publication the UCS concludes, 'A new ethic is required.' <http://www.ucsusa.org/about/1992-world-scientists.html> at 20 May 2009.

23 Bill McKibben, 'Because the World Needs to Know' (public lecture, University of Melbourne, 11 May 2009).

24 On feedback loops and the tipping point, see New Economic Foundation, '100 Months: Technical Note' (2008) <www.neweconomics.org> at 20 May 2009 (which calculates that 100 months from August 2008, atmospheric concentrations of greenhouse gases will begin to exceed a point whereby it will no longer be *likely* we will be able to avert potentially irreversible climate change).

25 See Mathis Wackernagel et al, 'Tracking the Ecological Overshoot of the Human Economy,' *Proceedings of the Academy of Science*, no 99 (2002).

26 An 'ecological footprint' is a measure of the amount of renewable and non-renewable ecologically productive land area required to support the resource demands and absorb the wastes of a given population or specific activity. See Wackernagel et al, above n 25. 'Carrying capacity' can be defined as the maximum population of a given species that can be supported indefinitely in a defined habitat without permanently impairing the productivity of that habitat. See William Rees, 'Revisiting Carrying Capacity: Area-Based Indicators of Sustainability', (1996) 17 *Population and Environment: A Journal of Interdisciplinary Studies* 3. See also, Donella Meadows et al, *The Limits to Growth: The 30 Year Update* (2004).

per cent.[27] Of similar concern, the United Nations Global Environment Outlook 2007 (GEO4) provides details on, among other things, the reality of climate change, reporting that 11 of the last 12 years (1995-2006) have been the hottest since 1850.[28] Furthermore, in 2005, as noted earlier, the United Nations 'Millennium Ecosystems Assessment' revealed that 60% of global ecosystem services are 'being degraded or used unsustainably,' resulting in 'substantial and largely irreversible loss in the diversity of life on Earth.'[29] Finally, the German Federal Ministry Report released in May 2008, the biggest assessment ever made of the economic impact of environmental damage, reported that the damage is already between 2.1 and 4.8 trillion US dollars per year (although very little of this cost is currently factored into any nation's GDP, meaning that we are not doing as well we might think we are).[30] **This last report and others like it are arguably of particular significance in that they undermine economic growth in ecological *and* economic terms.**[31]

If confronted honestly, reports such as these directly and fundamentally challenge mainstream attitudes to economic growth, because they show (among other things) that the advanced capitalist societies are already significantly over-consuming their share of Earth's resources, and so presumably should not be striving to grow their economies even more. And yet, even as the evidence of environmental degradation mounts, it seems that political leaders on both sides of the political spectrum (to varying degrees) are unwilling or unable to recognize any ecological limits to growth; at least, none that the privatization of nature, deregulation of markets, technological efficiency, or more economic growth will not solve.[32] As George Bush, Sr., expressed it, in words his son could understand and later repeat: 'Growth is the friend of the environment.'[33] The now formidable body of environmental research has rendered this view dangerously false.

---

27 Redefining Progress, 'World's Ecological Footprint Exceeds Biological Capacity by Nearly 40%' (2006) <http://www.rprogress.org/press/releases/060323_EFA.htm> at 20 May 2009.

28 United Nations Global Environment Outlook 4 (2007). See: <http://www.unep.org/geo/geo4/media/fact_sheets/Fact_Sheet_4_Climate_Change.pdf> at 20 May 2009.

29 See above n 2.

30 German Federal Ministry for the Environment and the European Commission, 'The Economics of Ecosystems and Biodiversity' (2008) <http://www.teebweb.org/> at 20 May 2009.

31 See also, Nicholas Stern, *The Economics of Climate Change: The Stern Review* (2006) (concluding that the benefits of strong, early action on climate change will considerably outweigh the overall costs). Stern argues that investing one per cent of global GDP must be invested to avoid the worse effects of climate change and that failure to do so could result in global GDP being up to twenty percent lower than it might otherwise be.

32 See generally, T L Anderson and D R Leal, *Free Market Environmentalism* (1991).

33 As quoted in Meadows et al, *Limits to Growth: The 30 Year Update* (2004) 204.

The science which indicates over-consumption in the West is all the more challenging in light of the fact that, in the poorest parts of the world today, almost three billion human beings are, by any humane standard, *under-consuming*.[34] The global challenge, therefore, can be stated as follows: 'To reach sustainability, humanity must increase the consumption levels of the world's poor, while at the same time reducing humanity's total ecological footprint.'[35] To make this situation more challenging still, the global population is expected to exceed nine billion by mid-century.[36] Moreover, we know that the high-impact 'consumer class' is fast expanding into many parts of global society.[37]

In terms of ecological damage, which tends to impact disproportionately on poorer nations,[38] this situation is extremely bleak. Obviously, it is also of deep humanitarian concern, especially when the gaze of future generations enters the equation.[39] My question, then, is this: Will more economic growth in the developed world help *solve* these great problems of our age or only *exacerbate* them? I suggest that the scientific studies, such as those considered above, now support the latter view, and since the existential threat they imply is about as serious as we could imagine, this is not evidence to treat casually.

A Brief History of Growth Scepticism

The sceptical attitude towards growth that I am advocating has its roots at least as far back as John Stuart Mill, who in 1848 asked: 'Towards what ultimate point is society tending by its industrial progress?'[40] This powerful question is significant for three reasons. First, because it acknowledges, implicitly, that

[34] World Bank Development Indicators, 'Poverty Data' (2008) at:

<www.siteresources.worldbank.org/DATASTATISTICS/Resources/WDI08supplement1216.pdf> at 20 May 2009.

[35] Meadows et al, *Limits to Growth: The 30 Year Update* (2004) xv.

[36] United Nations Department of Economic and Social Affairs, 'World Population Prospects' (2007) <http://www.un.org/esa/population/publications/wpp2006/English.pdf> at 20 May 2009.

[37] See WorldWatch Institute, *State of the World: The Consumer Society* (2004).

[38] Nicholas Stern, *The Economics of Climate Change: The Stern Review* (2006). See also, United Nations Development Program, *Human Development Report* (2007/8) 3 (using the term 'apocalyptic' to describe potential impact on the poor.)

[39] Lawrence B. Solum, 'To Our Children's Children: The Problem of Intergenerational Ethics' (2001) 35 *Loyola of LA L R* 163.

[40] J.S. Mill, *Principles of Political Economy: With Some of their Applications to Social Philosophy*, (1870).

industrial progress (or economic growth) is only of instrumental value and not of any intrinsic value;[41] second, because it raises the possibility that there might come a time when further economic growth no longer advances any worthwhile purposes; and third, and perhaps most importantly, because it prompts us to consider not only how much economic growth is *enough*, but also the prior question of what we want growth *for*.

Mill believed that if there came a time when economic growth stopped contributing to well-being (or began undermining those things upon which well-being depends), the most suitable form of government would be what he called 'the stationary state.' By this he meant a condition of zero growth in population and physical capital stock, but with continued improvement in technology and in what he called 'the art of living.'[42] Mill was warning posterity – us, it would seem – to respect the limits to growth before the consequences of going beyond those limits compelled respect, in one way or another.

Later, in 1967, the economist Ezra Mishan published *The Costs of Economic Growth*,[43] in which he condemned the growth model for assuming that economic growth could increase infinitely on a finite planet, and for assuming that increased consumption (or a higher 'standard of living') always meant a better 'quality of life.'[44] Mishan highlighted the fact that economic growth had *costs*, and he argued that those costs were beginning to outweigh the benefits. A similar critique, though with a closer environmentalist focus, was advanced in 1972 by the Club of Rome, in their treatise, *Limits to Growth*.[45] In 1976, another critique, this time with a sociological focus, was advanced by Fred Hirsch, in his text, *Social Limits to Growth*.[46]

Since the early 70s, ecological economist Herman Daly has built upon and significantly developed a number of these ideas.[47] Of particular relevance to this paper is the work he pioneered with J.B. Cobb developing a post-growth measure of progress, called the Index of Sustainable Economic Welfare

41 Ronald Dworkin has expressed a similar point in the following way: 'Money or its equivalent is useful so far as it enables someone to lead a more valuable, successful, happier, or more moral life. Anyone who counts it for more than that is a fetishist of little green paper.' Ronald Dworkin, 'Is Wealth a Value?', above n 16, 191.

42 Mill, above n 40.

43 Mishan, above n 21.

44 For insightful discussions of the notions of 'standard of living' and 'quality of life,' see Martha Nussbaum and Amartya Sen (eds.), *The Quality of Life: Studies in Development Economics* (1993).

45 Donella Meadows et al, *The Limits to Growth: The 30 Year Update* (2004).

46 Fred Hirsh, *The Social Limits to Growth* (1993, revised edition).

47 See Herman Daly, *Steady-State Economics* (1977) and *Beyond Growth: The Economics of Sustainable Development* (1996).

(ISEW).[48] As a model of progress, this index and others like it take into consideration important social and environmental factors that economic growth alone does not reflect. For example, the ISEW makes deductions from GDP for such things as resource depletion, pollution, income inequality, loss of leisure, etc, and makes additions for such things as public infrastructure, volunteering, and domestic work.[49] Merging environmentalist and economic perspectives, Daly argues that sustainable development in the developed world necessarily entails a radical shift away from 'growth economies' towards what he calls a 'steady-state economy.'[50] By this he means (updating and refining Mill) an economy that continues to develop in response to new technologies and changing cultural and market forces, but without growing in a bio-physical sense.[51]

More recently, forceful critiques of growth have come from such theorists as Clive Hamilton, Peter Victor, and Tim Jackson,[52] who variously argue that the process of getting richer is now, paradoxically, causing the very problems that we seem to think getting richer will solve. Attacking the fundamentals of the neoliberal growth project, these authors urge the advanced capitalist societies to begin exploring the possibility of prosperity without growth.

Some of the most rigorous and provocative expressions of growth scepticism have emerged over the last decade out of the Degrowth Movement in Europe. Regrettably, this rich literature has barely made an appearance in Anglo-Saxon academic or public dates,[53] although perhaps the tide may eventually turn as a

---

48 Herman Daly and John Cobb, *For the Common Good: Redirecting the Economy Toward Community, the Environment, and a Sustainable Future* (1989).

49 Other post-growth measures of progress include the Genuine Progress Indicator and The Human Development Index. These tend to suggest that many advanced capitalist societies have stopped progressing, in terms of genuine human well-being, despite continuing to get richer. For a review of some of the research, see Avner Offer, *The Challenge of Affluence: Self-Control and Wellbeing in the United States and Britain since 1950* (2006). See also, John Talberth, Clifford Cobb, and Noah Slattery, 'The Genuine Progress Indicator' (2006) <www.rprogress.org> at 20 May 2009; and Philip Lawn, 'A Theoretical Foundation to Support the ISEW, GPI, and other related indexes' (2003) *Ecological Economics* (August) 959-983.

50 Herman Daly, *Steady-State Economics* (1977).

51 In framing his arguments in biophysical terms, Daly acknowledges his debt to Nicolas Georgescu-Roegen, especially to the seminal text, *The Entropy Law and the Economic Process* (1971).

52 See Clive Hamilton, *Growth Fetish* (2003); Peter Victor, *Managing without Growth* (2008); and Tim Jackson, 'Prosperity without Growth?' (2009) <http://www.sd-commission.org.uk/publications/downloads/prosperity_without_growth_report.pdf> at 20 May 2009.

53 As late as 2008 Valerie Fournier noted that there were only three English-language articles on degrowth, beside a few articles by Serge Latouche published in the English Version of *Le*

result of the First International Degrowth Conference in Paris 2008, some of the proceedings from which are freely available online and predominately in English.[54]

Though not a unified doctrine by any means, an emerging consensus within the Degrowth Movement has resulted in a Declaration of Degrowth.[55] This document (to paraphrase) calls for a paradigm shift from the general and unlimited pursuit of economic growth to a concept of 'right-sizing' both global and national economies. At the global level, right-sizing means reducing the global ecological footprint (including carbon footprint) to a sustainable level. In countries where per capita footprint is greater than the sustainable global level, this right-sizing implies a reduction to this level through the process of voluntary economic contraction (i.e. degrowth).[56] In countries where severe poverty still remains, right-sizing implies increasing consumption to a level adequate for a decent life. This will involve increasing economic activity in some cases, but redistribution of income and wealth both within and between countries is a more essential part of the process.[57]

Responding to those 'free-market environmentalists' or 'technological optimists' in the mainstream who claim that there is no conflict between growth and sustainability (i.e. 'development'),[58] the Degrowth Movement points out that although techno-efficiency solutions have been widely applied, flows of material and energy (or *throughput*) are still increasing.[59] This increase in throughput despite the increases in efficiency is largely due to 'rebound effects,' as Francis Schneider neatly explains by way of example: 'a car that consumes less gasoline per km leads to financial savings that may be spent on longer car distances… A so-called secondary rebound exists when a house is better insulated and that reduced expenditure on heating is reinvested in buying a second car or travelling by plane.'[60] In short, efficiency 'creates revenue that can

---

Monde Diplomatique. See Valerie Fournier, 'Escaping from the Economy: The Politics of Degrowth' (2008) 28 *International Journal Sociology and International Research* 11/12 528-545.

54 See www.degrowth.net.

55 Ibid.

56 Serge Latouche, 'Degrowth Economics: Why Less Should Be Much More' (2004) *Le Monde Diplomatique* (English Ed., Nov.) <http://mondediplo.com/2006/01/13degrowth> at 20 May 2009.

57 New Economic Foundation, 'Growth Isn't Working: The Unbalanced Distribution of Benefits and Costs from Economic Growth' (2006) <http://www.neweconomics.org/> at 20 May 2009 (showing that First World growth is an ineffective response to poverty.)

58 Unpacking this view, see Wolfgang Sachs (ed.) *Development Dictionary* (1992).

59 See Francis Schneider, 'Macroscopic Rebound Effects as Argument for Economic Degrowth' in *Proceedings of the First International Degrowth Conference* (2008) <www.degrowth.net> at 20 May 2009.

60 Ibid 29.

be spent on the same (primary rebound) or other commodities (secondary rebounds).'[61] Efficiency, for this reason among others, is a fatally flawed solution to the problems of growth and over-consumption.

The tradition of growth scepticism outlined above, from Mill to 'degrowth,' may strike some as an unspeakable heresy and perhaps be dismissed in advance of honest consideration. But what seems clear is that if we are genuinely committed to the idea of a sustainable society – of each generation of life on Earth meeting its needs without jeopardizing the prospects of future generations to meet their needs[62] – then the pursuit of more economic growth by those nations which are already consuming an unsustainable share is ethically objectionable. Time has come, that is, for the over-consuming nations to give up the pursuit of growth, for it is looking ever-more like an unambiguous act of violence.

There have been and are other growth sceptics,[63] arising out of various disciplines and focusing on different issues, but the focal point of this paper concerns various issues that arise when *property rights* are considered within a post-growth framework – the framework that I claim best represents the position implicit to Earth Jurisprudence. With an admittedly broad brush, I will now bring this paper to a head by offering a few thoughts on how the property systems of advanced capitalism might change – and how our thinking about those systems might change – and with what consequences, if economic growth were to lose its privileged position as the touchstone of policy success.

Property beyond Growth

---

61 Ibid.

62 For international agreements on sustainability, see 'Agenda 21' and the 'Rio Declaration on Environment and Development' (1992), both of which were reaffirmed at the World Summit on Sustainable Development (WSSD) held in Johannesburg, South Africa, in 2002. For an important new discussion of the meaning of sustainability, see Klaus Bosselmann, *The Principle of Sustainability* (2008).

63 A sample of further examples across various disciplines include, John K. Galbraith, *The Affluent Society* (1958); Robert Theobald, *The Challenge of Abundance* (1961); E.F. Schumacher, *Small is Beautiful: A Study of Economics as if People Mattered* (1973); Richard Easterlin, 'Does Economic Growth Improve the Human Lot? Some Empirical Evidence' in Paul A. David and Melvin W. Reder, eds., *Nations and Households in Economic Growth: Essays in Honor of Moses Abramovitz* (1974); Paul Wachtel, *The Poverty of Affluence* (1982); Ted Trainer, 'Recognizing Limits to Growth: a challenge to political economy' (2002) 50 *Journal of Australian Political Economy* 2, 163-78; Bill McKibben, *Deep Economy* (2007).

We have seen that the 'growth model of progress' assumes that the overriding objective of a property system is to facilitate economic growth as efficiently as possible, a goal which is thought to be best achieved when 'unqualified' property rights are traded in 'free markets.' It is my contention that by neglecting the problems of over-consumption and the costs of economic growth, this neoliberal perspective on property is naively entrenched in an outdated context and dangerously informed by an outdated set of values. The ecological crisis, in particular, as well as unprecedented Western affluence, places us in a context so radically different to that of earlier generations that the justifiability of inherited property rights, shaped for a different age, must not be taken for granted. Indeed, they should be subjected to a fundamental reassessment and, if need be, a fundamental revision. Justification, after all, as historicists from Hegel to Foucault have shown, is context-dependent. And things have changed.

Looking beyond the 'growth model,' a post-growth property system would be one in which property rules, market structures, and tax policies were designed explicitly to achieve welfare-enhancing objectives more specific than the efficient growth of GDP. These more specific objectives would include protecting the environment or eliminating poverty, and in pursuing these objectives the efficient growth of GDP (or lack thereof) would be treated as a by-product of secondary importance.[64] In essence, s*ufficiency* would be privileged over *efficiency*, and in over-consuming regions of the world this would need to involve planned economic contraction, or 'degrowth.'

Reforming Western property systems in the spirit of degrowth could be initiated in a variety of ways. The following proposals, rather than aiming to grow the economy, would aim to promote sufficiency and sustainability, resist over-consumption, foster community and democracy, protect the vulnerable, and distribute wealth more broadly.

Proposed Reforms: (1) Unconditionally guarantee a minimal, state-funded, Basic Income for all; (2) Establish a system of progressive income tax that culminates in a democratically determined 'maximum wage;' (3) Facilitate the emergence of more communitarian and ecologically sensitive corporate structures, such as Worker Cooperatives or Employee Stock Ownership Plans; (4) Regulate, with explicit reference to the common good, powerful and socially

---

64 On how growth is an obstacle to achieving mores specific welfare enhancing objectives, see the New Economics Foundation Report, 'Unintended Consequences: How the efficiency agenda erodes local public services and a new public benefit model to restore them' (2007) <www.neweconomics.org> at 20 May 2009. See also P. Victor and G. Rosenbluth, 'Managing Without Growth' (2007) 61 *Ecological Economics* 492.

influential 'private' institutions, such as banks, mass media, and mega-corporations; (5) Impose stricter and more precautionary environmental rules on land use and development, such as prohibiting 'intensive' land use and other forms of unsustainable production/manufacture; (6) Devise land-use rules that are more socially beneficial, such as those which would curtail 'urban sprawl' or protect common spaces and assets; (7) Increase taxes (especially inheritance taxes, luxury taxes, and wealth taxes) as (a) a corrective/redistributive measure; (b) to channel the forces of money toward socially and environmentally beneficial places; and (c) to better fund public services (health, education, public transport, the arts, foreign aid, etc.); (8) Establish more 'green' taxes to internalize externalities and price commodities at their 'true cost.' All this is merely suggestive of a vague (and no doubt controversial) alternative framework. My aim here is obviously not to provide a blueprint.

Although such reforms may well slow economic growth – even to the point of 'degrowth' – and thereby not maximize a nation's material 'standard of living,' my underlying thesis is that the reforms would at the same time increase 'quality of life.'[65] Such a thesis, of course, is incommensurable with the 'growth model of progress,' since that model effectively conflates 'standard of living' and 'quality of life.'[66] But as the ecological (and social)[67] critiques of growth make clear, it is wrong to conflate those very distinct concepts.

---

[65] It would be proper to insist that we ought to seek sustainability even if this would *reduce* 'quality of life' and involve some uncompensated sacrifice. While that can hardly be denied, I would argue that reducing consumption will lead to an overall benefit to most people embedded in consumer culture. See generally, Samuel Alexander (ed.), *Voluntary Simplicity: The Poetic Alternative to Consumer Culture* (2009).

[66] See Nussbaum and Sen, above n 44.

[67] See Samuel Alexander, 'Law, Economics, and the Social Critique of Growth: An Inquiry into the Correlation between Material Wealth and Well-being' (unpublished manuscript on file with author). In this manuscript I review the large and credible body of social research which examines the correlation between material wealth and well-being. The research broadly establishes: (1) that individuals in rich nations report higher levels of well-being than individuals in poor nations, but that rich nations are not much better off, if at all, than nations of moderate material wealth (i.e. with per capita incomes of US$10-15,000); (2) that, within a nation, rich individuals report higher levels of well-being than poor individuals, but that rich individuals are not much better off, if at all, than individuals of moderate material wealth; and (3) that, over time, getting richer makes people better off *up to a point*, but once moderate material wealth has been attained, getting richer makes little, if any, difference to well-being. There is also evidence which indicates that, once moderate wealth has been attained, increases in material wealth can, at times, even be *negatively* correlated with well-being. See also, Ed Diener and Martin Seligman, "Beyond Money: Toward an Economy of Well-Being," *Psychological Science in the Public Interest* 5(1) (2004) 1 (reviewing over 150 studies assessing the correlation between financial wealth and well-being); Robert E. Lane, *The Loss of Happiness in Market Democracies* (2000); Tim Kasser, *The High Price of Materialism* (2002); Richard Layard,

I acknowledge that any transition to a post-growth economy would require extensive structural reform of the property system over time. And I accept that this will give rise to the culturally powerful charge of 'inefficiency,' always levelled at those who propose 'interventionalist' or 'regulatory' structural reform of the property system.[68] But I believe that this objection, due to its very nature, loses much of its force when considered in light of the ecological critique of growth. In short, the 'inefficiency' objection is that post-growth reform of the property system would not maximize economic growth, since it would involve interfering in the supposedly 'efficient' operation of so-called 'free markets'. Based on the environmental (and social) science – even based on the economics! – the post-growth response is that not maximizing economic growth is partly or beside the point. In a sense, then, I would respond to the objection by embracing it, not as an indictment but as a defence.[69]

In summary, I have argued that when an economy has grown so large that it exceeds the regenerative and absorptive capacities of Earth's ecosystems, then lawmakers ought to initiate a 'degrowth' process of planned economic contraction. I have tried to show that this argument has particular relevance to the jurisprudence of property, and I hope that my preliminary contribution may provoke some interest in how growth scepticism might impact, not only on property law, but on legal issues more broadly. It is my contention that legal scholars will find in growth scepticism the seeds of much fruitful and important research.

Conclusion: Nature beyond Property

The poet-philosopher, Henry David Thoreau, was deeply troubled by the orthodox economic conception of nature and particularly sensitive to its

Happiness: Lessons from a New Science (2005); Bruno Frey and Alois Stutzer, *Happiness and Economics* (2002). The social research suggests that rich nations have already gone beyond the 'material threshold' beyond which more income does not contribute much to well-being. And this 'social critique' makes growth as an economic policy seem not just wasteful but counter-productive.

68 For example, see Richard Epstein, 'Why Restrain Alienation?' (1985) 85 *Colum. L Rev* 970 (arguing that no deviations from free-market alienability are permitted unless they are required by 'efficiency').

69 I have explored some of these ideas further in 'Property beyond Growth: Toward a Politics of Voluntary Simplicity,' in David Grinlinton and Prue Taylor (ed.), *Property Rights and Sustainability: The Evolution of Property Rights to Meet Ecological Challenges* (2010).

limitations. 'If a man walk in the woods for love of them half of each day, he is in danger of being regarded as a loafer. But if he spends his days as a speculator, shearing off those woods and making the earth bald before her time, he is deemed an industrious and enterprising citizen.'[70] To treat nature as a 'resource' for human consumption is one way to look at the world. But Earth Jurisprudence, through its Thoreauvian lens, sees nature very differently, as having a value in itself. The Transcendentalist, Ralph Waldo Emerson, expressed this reverential attitude beautifully in his essay 'Nature':

> I see the spectacle of morning from the hilltop over against my house, from daybreak to sunrise, with emotions which an angel might share. The long slender bars of cloud float like fishes in the sea of crimson light. From the earth, as a shore, I look out into that silent sea. I seem to partake its rapid transformations; the active enchantment reaches my dust, and I dilate and conspire with the morning wind.[71]

In the same essay, he noted: 'In good health, the air is a cordial of incredible virtue. Crossing a bare common, in snow puddles, at twilight, under a clouded sky, without having in my thoughts any occurrence of special good fortune, I have enjoyed a perfect exhilaration. I am glad to the brink of fear.'[72]

My point in citing these passages is that there is *something* in the experience of nature, of 'the Wild,' which ought not to be and, indeed, cannot be 'valued' according to its price in the market, or boxed up and traded as a mere commodity. The fact that this *something* defies precise analytical expression or economic valuation does not mean that it is of no 'value.' On the contrary, it may just mean that it is *priceless* and thus deserving of our utmost care and respect; if we can muster the humility, even our reverence.

---

[70] Henry David Thoreau, 'Life without Principle' (1854) in Carl Bode, ed., *The Portable Thoreau* (1982) 633.
[71] Ralph Waldo Emerson, 'Nature' (1836) in Carl Bode, ed., *The Portable Emerson* (1981) 14.
[72] Ibid, 10.

The True Cost of Economic Rights Jurisprudence

Max McCann*

> [A] man has a property in his opinions and the free communication of them. . . . In a word, as a man is said to have a right to his property, he may be equally said to have a property in his rights. Where an excess of power prevails, property of no sort is duly respected. No man is safe in his opinions, his person, his faculties, or his possessions.[1]

INTRODUCTION

In contemporary political discourse, rights are often discussed as belonging to one of two exclusive camps – the individual rights and the economic rights.[2] In this context, individual rights conjure images of being free in one's person, including such rights as reproductive freedom, freedom of expression, and a right to privacy.[3] Meanwhile, economic rights connote freedom in wealth and industry, such as property rights; freedom of contract; and a right to earn, save, and exchange capital freely.[4] Interestingly, this distinction translates into terms

* *Assistant Corporation Counsel*, New York City Law Department; Brooklyn Law School class of 2008. The author would like to thank Professor Jason Mazzone, Professor Claire Kelly, Clark Neily and the Institute for Justice, Roger Pilon, and Joseph Becker. The views expressed herein are those of the author and not those of the New York City Law Department.

1 James Madison, *Property*, NATIONAL GAZETTE, Mar. 29, 1792, at 171, *reprinted in* 4 LETTERS AND OTHER WRITINGS OF JAMES MADISON 480 (1865).

2 Economic rights and individual rights are loosely construed terms of art, and there is admitted variance in the use of this vernacular. Economic rights may be coined, among other things, "property rights," "fiscal rights," or "proprietarian rights." Likewise, individual rights are known to go by such epithets as "personal rights," "political rights," or "social rights," to name a few. On a more basic level, the term "rights" itself will be used throughout this Article to discuss the theoretical concept of an asserted liberty interest, whether or not the Court has recognized it as a right. The mere labeling of an asserted liberty interest as a "right" should not be mistaken for advocacy of the Court's recognition of this right. Furthermore, the question of whether a liberty interest that is not recognized and protected by the government is a "right" is beyond the scope of this article.

3 Kathleen M. Sullivan, *Unconstitutional Conditions*, 102 HARV. L. REV. 1413, 1492 (1989).

4 ECONOMIC RIGHTS vii (Ellen F. Paul et al. eds., Cambridge Univ. Press 1992) (defining economic rights as the ability to "use, possess, exchange and otherwise dispose of property."); Randy E. Barnett, *The Function of Several Property and Freedom of Contract*, in ECONOMIC RIGHTS, at 62-94.

of partisan politics with some measure of accuracy. Modern liberals[5] typically champion individual rights, while advocating deference to the legislature on all matters economic.[6] In contrast, conservatives show a marked preference for freedoms of the economic sort, while supporting regulation over much individual behavior.[7] Proving that the judicial system is a political being, this divide has permeated our modern legal jurisprudence. To be certain, one need only look to the unbroken line of U.S. Supreme Court cases applying different levels of scrutiny to economic regulation as opposed to laws constituting a prior restraint on speech.[8]

This Article, however, will argue that economic rights cannot be neatly distinguished from noneconomic rights. More so, this Article will show that, due to an inextricable link between the two, the very attempt to distinguish and adjudicate the two spheres separately has had pronounced, unintended consequences on individual rights. Section I of this Article provides a brief history of the bifurcation of rights into economic and individual groupings. Section II will then highlight several modern political issues, such as campaign finance law and commercial speech regulation, which blur the distinction between "economic" and "individual" rights. Section III will show that the very attempt to adjudicate claims of economic rights separately from other rights has had collateral, unaccounted-for effects on many rights more properly considered individual in nature. Finally, Section IV will argue that this

---

5 The labels "conservative" and "liberal" are used in their modern, popular sense with full recognition that both are sweeping caricatures that fail to encompass the complexity of the philosophy they purport to describe. For example, a growing number of liberal authors and scholars recognize that protections for economic functions are vital in modern society. *See, e.g.*, Mark Tushnet, *The Newer Property: Suggestion for the Revival of Substantive Due Process*, 1975 SUP. CT. REV. 261, 273-77 (criticizing the two-step analysis of due process claims). Nonetheless, as generalizations, they contain some degree of truth and provide valuable insight into the political perspectives of our time.

6 William S. Maddox and Stuart A. Lilie, *Beyond Liberal and Conservative* (Washington: Cato Institute, 1984) at 5; Richard Levy, *Escaping Lochner's Shadow: Toward a Coherent Jurisprudence of Economic Rights*, 73 N.C. L. REV. 329, 361-64 (1995). As an illustration, the mission statement of the National Lawyers Guild, a liberal jurist association, includes the following mantra: "to the end that human rights shall be regarded as more sacred than property interests." http://www.nlg.org/about/aboutus.htm.

7 Levy, *supra* note 6, at 342-48. Think tax reform, privatizing Social Security, and industry deregulation on the one hand and the Defense of Marriage Act on the other.

8 *See* Peter Linzer, *The Carolene Products Footnote And The Preferred Position of Individual Rights: Louis Lusky And John Hart Ely vs. Harlan Fiske Stone*, 12 CONST. COMMENT. 277 (1995). *Compare* Williamson v. Lee Optical of Okla., 348 U.S. 483 (1955) (declaring that state legislatures may pursue economic regulation with impunity, even with actions that are "unwise, improvident.") *with* Nebraska Press Association v. Stuart, 427 U.S. 539 (1976) (unanimously declaring that prior restraints on speech are presumptively unconstitutional).

distinction between individual and economic rights is somewhat fallacious and that the only way to provide meaningful protection to either is through equal reverence to both.

I. A BRIEF HISTORY OF THE BIFURCATION OF RIGHTS

Throughout the ages, Anglo-American jurisprudence has been concerned in large part with protecting economic rights.[9] Early constitutional law

[9] Regal respect for property interests in the English common law can be traced back as far as the Charter of Henry I, which predates the Magna Carta by more than a century. Bernard H. Siegan, ECONOMIC LIBERTIES AND THE CONSTITUTION 1 (1980) [hereinafter Siegan, ECONOMIC LIBERTIES]. Two of the three paragraphs of this charter relate to property -- eliminating high redemption rates to heirs of land and returning property taken after the death of Henry's brother and predecessor, Rufus. *Id.* The Magna Carta of 1215 went even further by making the prototypical pledge not to deprive innocent people of life, liberty, or *property*. Arthur R. Hogue, ORIGINS OF THE COMMON LAW 112 (1966). John Locke's Two Treatises of Government, eminently influential on the English common law, is replete with assertions that the chief end of civil society is the preservation of property. John Locke, TWO TREATISES OF GOVERNMENT 141, 145, 165, 261 (Peter Laslett ed., Cambridge Univ. Press 1988) (1690); Karen Iversen Vaughn, *The Economic Background to Locke's Two Treatises of Government*, *in* JOHN LOCKE'S TWO TREATISES OF GOVERNMENT 119 (Edward J. Harpham ed., 1992) ("Indeed, the whole tenor of Locke's arguments is suffused with economic presuppositions."). By some accounts, security of economic rights was the motivating force behind the development of English common law, which was the single most imminent influence on the development of American jurisprudence. Bernard H. Siegan, *Protecting Economic Liberties*, 6 CHAP. L. REV. 43 (2003) [hereinafter Siegan, *Protecting Economic Liberties*]. That the emerging American legal system incorporated these protections is no surprise, as the American Revolution was in large part a response to economic oppression, such as the Stamp Act of 1765, the Townshend Revenue Act of 1767, and the Tea Tax of 1773. H. Commager, DOCUMENTS OF AMERICAN HISTORY, 104 (8th ed. 1968); see also, Jennifer Nedelsky, PRIVATE PROPERTY AND THE LIMITS OF AMERICAN CONSTITUTIONALISM 92 (1990) ("The great focus of the Framers was the security of basic rights, property in particular, not the implementation of political liberty."). Indeed, the Virginia Declaration of Rights, drafted by George Mason in 1776, extols the "inherent right" of "acquiring and possessing property" in its very first section. *Preamble of the Virginia Constitution*, PENNSYLVANIA GAZETTE, June 12, 1776, *reprinted in* Pauline Maier, AMERICAN SCRIPTURE: MAKING THE DECLARATION OF INDEPENDENCE 126-27 (1997). This document was a template for many subsequent state bills of rights and is thought to have influenced Thomas Jefferson when drafting the United States Declaration of Independence as well as James Madison when drafting the Bill of Rights. Madison himself showed a prophetic concern for the disparate treatment of rights, declaring "I see no reason why the rights of property which chiefly bears the burden of Government and is so much an object of Legislation should not be respected as well as personal rights in the choice of Rulers." James Madison, 8 PAPERS OF JAMES MADISON 353 (Robert A. Rutland & William M.E. Rachal eds., 1973). Some even suggest that Jefferson might have substituted "pursuit of happiness" in the Declaration of Independence in place of Mason's "property" because he regarded "pursuit of happiness" as "a kind of generic term for a bundle of rights that included property rights." David N. Mayer, THE CONSTITUTIONAL THOUGHT OF THOMAS JEFFERSON 78 (1994). Finally, the United States

jurisprudence viewed economic regulation with almost unshakable disapproval,[10] striking down restrictions on the right to contract,[11] limitations on working hours,[12] barriers to market entry,[13] regulation of prices,[14] regulatory takings,[15] mandates on wages,[16] and anti-trust laws.[17] During the 1930s, however, the Court faced enormous political pressure[18] to abandon its previous proclivity for economic rights.[19] Even before the onset of the Great Depression, President Franklin D. Roosevelt championed sweeping regulation of many industries, a plan he later coined the New Deal.[20] Much to President Roosevelt's frustration, the Court presented a formidable obstacle in implementing the New Deal;[21] between 1934 and 1936, the Hughes Court

---

Constitution of course promises to protect "life, liberty and property." U.S. CONST. amend. XIV, § 1.

10 Siegan, ECONOMIC LIBERTY, *supra* note 9, at 178-79.

11 *See, e.g.*, Allgeyer v. Louisiana, 165 U.S. 578 (1897) (unanimously striking down prohibition on contracting with out of state insurance carriers as a violation of due process); Central of Ga. Ry. Co. v. Wright, 248 U.S. 525, 527 (1919) (finding revocation of state charter invalid as violation of the Contract Clause).

12 *See, e.g.*, Lochner v. New York, 198 U.S. 45 (1905) (striking down regulation of the number of hours that bakers could work on substantive due process grounds).

13 *See, e.g.*, New State Ice Co. v. Liebmann, 285 U.S. 262 (1932); Yick Wo v. Hopkins, 118 U.S. 356, 370 (1886) (striking down a licensing scheme for laundry businesses as a violation of equal protection, noting "[t]he very idea that one man may be compelled to hold his life, or the means of living, or any material right essential to the enjoyment of life, at the mere will of another, seems to be intolerable in any country where freedom prevails, as being the essence of slavery itself").

14 *See, e.g.*, Nebbia v. New York, 291 U.S. 502, 515 (1934); A.L.A. Schechter Poultry Corp. v. U.S., 295 U.S. 495, 542 (1935).

15 Pennsylvania Coal v. Mahon, 260 U.S. 393, 414-15 (1922) (finding a requirement to leave coal in place totally destroyed mineral owner's interests and, thus, was a taking).

16 *See, e.g.*, Adkins v. Children's Hospital, 261 U.S. 525 (1923).

17 *See, e.g.*, U.S. v. E.C. Knight, 156 U.S. 1 (1895) (finding sugar refining to be manufacturing not commerce, and therefore, not subject to the Interstate Commerce Act).

18 William E. Leuchtenburg, THE SUPREME COURT REBORN: THE CONSTITUTIONAL REVOLUTION IN THE AGE OF ROOSEVELT 169 (1995); 2 Bruce A. Ackerman, WE THE PEOPLE: TRANSFORMATIONS 306 (1998) (referring to soon-to-be President Roosevelt's agenda as an "irresistible force [] on a collision course with an immoveable object"). *But see*, G. EDWARD WHITE, THE CONSTITUTION AND THE NEW DEAL 5 (2000) (arguing that the jurisprudential change came not from political pressures, but from a conceptual response to several factors in modern society).

19 Siegan, ECONOMIC LIBERTIES, *supra* note 9, at 184-85 (attributing the pre-New Deal Court's opposition to economic regulation to a belief in the "efficacy of Adam Smith's celebrated observations that the wealth of a nation largely depends on privately created production").

20 *Id.* at 191-195. Professor Siegan notes that, "[i]t is a myth that the New Deal was adopted as a result of the Great Depression." *Id.* at 194.

21 Siegan, ECONOMIC LIBERTIES, *supra* note 9, at 107 (noting that from 1890 to 1936 the Court invalidated an average of 8.6 congressional acts per year).

struck down some sixteen of its acts.[22] In 1938, however, the Court blinked.[23] In the totemic *United States v. Carolene Products*[24] decision, the Supreme Court set forth a mandate of legislative deference that would forever change judicial review of both individual and economic rights.

Carolene Products considered the constitutionality of the Filled Milk Act of 1923,[25] "which prohibit[ed] the shipment in interstate commerce of skimmed milk compounded with any fat or oil other than milk fat, so as to resemble milk or cream."[26] The Carolene Products Company challenged the act, asserting that it was not within Congress' power to regulate commerce and, thus, a violation of the powers reserved to the States.[27]

Justice Stone dismissed these arguments, citing a need to defer to Congress' findings on the injurious nature of filled milk.[28] But in the famous footnote four, the Court observed that some legislation may warrant a "more exacting judicial scrutiny."

---

[22] Henry J. Abraham, THE JUDICIAL PROCESS: AN INTRODUCTORY ANALYSIS OF THE COURTS OF THE UNITED STATES, ENGLAND, AND FRANCE 299-320 (7th ed., 1998).

[23] President Roosevelt's "Court packing plan" may have contributed to the Court's change of heart, although there is some dispute about the significance of Roosevelt's threat. Richard Levy, *Escaping Lochner's Shadow: Toward a Coherent Jurisprudence of Economic Rights*, 73 N.C. L. REV. 329 (1995); Daniel A. Farber, *Who Killed Lochner?*, 90 GEO. L.J. 985, 997 (2002) (reviewing G. EDWARD WHITE, THE CONSTITUTION AND THE NEW DEAL (2000)). Regardless of the effect, if any, of the Court packing plan, President Roosevelt was able to appoint eight new Justices during his twelve years in office, which no doubt contributed to the ideological shift in the Court. Siegan, ECONOMIC LIBERTIES, *supra* note 9, at 175.

[24] 304 U.S. 144 (1938). The Carolene Products Company was indicted for shipping in interstate commerce packages of "Milnut," a compound of skim milk and coconut oil. U.S. v. Carolene Prods., 7 F.Supp. 500, 501 (S.D. Ill. 1934).

[25] 21 U. S. C. §§ 61-63 (1923). Professor Geoffrey Miller has referred to the Filled Milk Act as "an utterly unprincipled example of special interest legislation." Geoffrey P. Miller, *The True Story of Carolene Products*, 1987 SUP. CT. REV. 397, 398. The legislation, according to Professor Miller, was supported by various farmer associations: breed groups, county, state, and national political organizations; dairy newspapers; agricultural colleges and universities; granges; and dairy promotional organizations. These dairy interests were threatened by filled milk products, which could be sold for a cheaper price than pure dairy products. Thus, the statute had more to do with driving small producers out of the market than its purported purpose of protecting consumers from what essentially amounts to skim milk. The statute also disadvantaged the working class and poor people, who were deprived of a healthful, nutritious, and low cost food. *Id.* at 399.

[26] 21 U.S.C. § 61(c) (1923); 304 U.S. at 145-46.

[27] 304 U.S. at 146-47. The Carolene Products Company also argued that the Act constituted a denial of equal protection and due process in violation of the Fifth Amendment. *Id.*

[28] *Id.* at 154.

> There may be narrower scope for operation of the presumption of constitutionality when legislation appears on its face to be within a specific prohibition of the Constitution, such as those of the first ten Amendments . . . . It is unnecessary to consider now whether legislation which restricts those political processes which can ordinarily be expected to bring about repeal of undesirable legislation, is to be subjected to more exacting judicial scrutiny under the general prohibitions of the Fourteenth Amendment . . . . Nor need we enquire . . . whether prejudice against discrete and insular minorities may be a special condition, which tends seriously to curtail the operation of those political processes ordinarily to be relied upon to protect minorities, and which may call for a correspondingly more searching judicial inquiry.[29]

In other words, the Court should exercise a pronounced level of deference to the legislature's wisdom, except where the allegedly offensive regulation infringes upon a fundamental right or discriminates against a "discrete and insular minority." It is a framework of constitutional presumption with exceptions of "more searching judicial inquiry."[30]

Although only dicta, this footnote has had the effect of establishing a hierarchy among asserted rights.[31] While the Ninth Amendment promises that "[t]he enumeration in the Constitution of certain rights shall not be construed to deny or disparage others retained by the people[,]"[32] the jurisprudence of *Carolene*

[29] *Id.* at 153, n.4.

[30] In a notable line of history, several famous subsequent cases were decided in agreement with *Carolene Products*, such as *Nebbia v. New York*, 291 U.S. 502 (1934), *West Coast Hotel v. Parrish*, 300 U.S. 100 (1941), and *Williamson v. Lee Optical Co.*, 348 U.S. 483 (1955). For a thorough treatment of this period *see, e.g.*, Siegan, ECONOMIC LIBERTIES, *supra* note 9, at 107-75. These cases were astonishingly successful in eviscerating economic rights, leading Professor McCloskey to comment that "it is hard to think of another instance when the Court so thoroughly and quickly demolished a constitutional doctrine of such far-reaching significance." Robert G. McCloskey, *Economic Due Process and the Supreme Court: An Exhumation and Reburial*, 1962 SUP. CT. REV. 34, 36.

[31] *See, e.g.*, Braunfeld v. Brown, 366 U.S. 599, 611-13 (1960) (Brennan, J., concurring in part, dissenting in part) (noting the preferential slot reserved for religious freedom). "The honored place of religious freedom in our constitutional hierarchy, suggested long ago by the argument of counsel in Permoli v. Municipality, and foreshadowed by a prescient footnote in United States v. Carolene Products Co. . . . must now be taken to be settled." *Id.*

[32] U.S. CONST. amend. IX.

Products has had precisely that effect.[33] Under this framework, the Court affords a more searching level of scrutiny to legislation affecting "fundamental" rights, while examining legislation affecting "nonfundamental" rights for mere perceptions of reasonableness.[34] [35] Predictably, favored rights, such as the

---

[33] *See e.g.*, Randy E. Barnett, *The Ninth Amendment: It Means What It Says*, 85 TEX. L. REV. 1, 21-80 (2006) (arguing for a common sense interpretation of the Ninth Amendment supported by crucial pieces of historical evidence, such as Madison's Bill of Rights speech, Roger Sherman's Draft Bill of Rights, and the Virginia Debates over the Ninth Amendment). The Ninth Amendment, Professor Barnett notes, "specifically negates the judicial philosophy adopted in the first paragraph of the famous Footnote Four of United States v. Carolene Products Co." *Id.* at 14.

[34] ERWIN CHEMERINSKY, CONSTITUTIONAL LAW, PRINCIPLES AND POLICIES, 625, 792 (3d. ed. 2006). In a decision that presaged this movement, Nebbia v. New York, 291 U.S. 502 (1934), the Court argued for the disparate treatment of economic rights. "So far as the requirement of due process is concerned . . . a state is free to adopt whatever economic policy may reasonably be deemed to promote public welfare . . . ." *Id.* at 537.

[35] The rights outside of the specific provisions of the Bill of Rights that the Court has found fundamental is a relatively short list, including the right to marry, Loving v. Virginia, 388 U.S. 1 (1967); the right to procreate, Skinner v. Oklahoma, 316 U.S. 535, 536 (1942); the right of parental custody of children, Santosky v. Kramer, 455 U.S. 745, 753 (1982); the right to control the upbringing of children, Meyer v. Nebraska, 262 U.S. 390 (1923), Pierce v. Society of Sisters, 268 U.S. 510 (1925); the right to keep one's family together, Moore v. City of East Cleveland, 431 U.S. 494 (1977); the right to marital privacy and to purchase and use contraceptives, Griswold v. Connecticut, 381 U.S. 479 (1965), Eisenstadt v. Baird, 405 U.S. 438 (1972); to bodily integrity, Rochin v. California, 342 U.S. 165 (1952); the right to abortion, Roe v. Wade, 410 U.S. 113 (1973); the right to travel, United States v. Guest, 383 U.S. 745 (1966); and the right to vote, Reynolds v. Simms, 377 U.S. 533, 555 (1964). Washington v. Glucksberg, 521 U.S. 702, 720 (1997) (collecting cases).

There is much debate about which rights *should* be found fundamental under the Due Process Clause. *See, e.g.*, Robert H. Bork, THE TEMPTING OF AMERICA (1990); Mark Tushnet, RED, WHITE, AND BLUE: A CRITICAL ANALYSIS OF CONSTITUTIONAL LAW (1988); John Hart Ely, DEMOCRACY AND DISTRUST (1980); Michael J. Perry, THE CONSTITUTION, THE COURTS, AND HUMAN RIGHTS (1982). Some argue that only those rights specifically mentioned or clearly implicit in the text of the Constitution are properly labeled fundamental. Ely, *supra*, at 1. This view is generally labeled originalism. Still, others argue that courts should go beyond the four corners of the Constitution when deciding what constitutes a fundamental right. *Id.* Predictably, this view is labeled nonoriginalism.

Other theories are also advanced for determining whether a right is fundamental. For example, moderate originalists believe courts should apply the framers' general intent, but not necessarily follow strict adherence to their exact views. *See, e.g.*, Paul Brest, *The Misconceived Quest for the Original Understanding*, 60 B. U. L. REV. 204, 205 (1980). Professor Lessig argues that the debate should be phrased in terms of "fidelity" to the historical understandings. *See, e.g.,* Lawrence Lessig, *Fidelity in Translation*, 71 TEX. L. REV. 1165 (1993); Lawrence Lessig, *Understanding Changed Readings: Fidelity and Theory*, 47 STAN. L. REV. 395 (1995); Michael Klarman, *Antifidelity*, 70 S. CAL. L. REV. 381 (1997); Symposium, *Fidelity in Constitutional Theory*, 65 FORDHAM L. REV. 1247 (1997). Some argue that courts should only recognize nontextual fundamental rights that further the goals of adequate representation and perfecting the political process. Ely, *supra*, at 1. Others would argue that courts should use principles of natural law in deciding which rights will

freedom of speech, are drafted into the "fundamental" camp,[36] while economic rights are cast into the disfavored "nonfundamental" group.[37] Although protections for economic rights may be found within the text of the Constitution,[38] the jurisprudence of the Progressive Era effectively demoted economic rights to the status of a "poor relation."[39] This court-conceived double standard[40] is the judicial embodiment of the individual/economic rights distinction.

The mechanics of legislative deference is as follows: If the right in question has been identified as nonfundamental, or if the legislation does not implicate a suspect minority, the Court applies the least searching level of scrutiny – the rational basis test.[41] To survive, the legislation must only be rationally related to a legitimate government interest.[42] The rational basis test, as formulated by modern courts, is succinctly described in *FCC v. Beach Communications*.[43] Under this test, the Court will uphold legislation "if there is any reasonably conceivable state of facts that could provide a rational basis" for it.[44] Such

---

receive fundamental status. *See, e.g.*, Harry V. Jaffa, ORIGINAL INTENT AND THE FRAMERS OF THE CONSTITUTION (1994). Some would argue that courts should recognize fundamental rights supported by strong moral consensus among society. *See, e.g.*, Harry H Wellington, *Common Law Rules and Constitutional Double Standards: Some Notes on Adjudication*, 83 YALE L. J. 221, 284 (1973). At times, the Court articulates the definition of a fundamental right as those "deeply rooted in our Nation's history and tradition." Moore v. City of East Cleveland, 431 U.S. 494, 503 (1977). But in practice, this definition does little to predict which rights the courts may find fundamental. Not only is there difficulty in ascertaining what amount of tradition is sufficient, there is also the question of at what level of abstraction the asserted right will be described. CHEMERINSKY, *supra* note 34, at 795. For example, a parent's right to control visitation times of grandparents may be stated as just that. Or it may be framed as a right to determine the upbringing of one's children. Naturally, the more specifically the right is described, the harder it will be to find a history and tradition of its protection. *Id.*

36 CHEMERINSKY, *supra* note 34, at 792.

37 *Id.* at 625.

38 *See, e.g.*, U.S. CONST. amend. XIV, § 1 (guaranteeing the protection of "life, liberty and property."); U.S. CONST. art. I, § 10, cl. 1 ("No State shall . . . pass any Law impairing the Obligation of Contracts. . . .")

39 Dolan v. City of Tigard, 512 U.S. 374, 392 (1994).

40 Henry J. Abraham and Barbara A. Perry, FREEDOM AND THE COURT: CIVIL RIGHTS AND LIBERTIES IN THE UNITED STATES 11 (8th ed. 2003).

41 *See, e.g.*, Williamson v. Lee Optical, 348 U.S. 483 (1955). In contrast, if the examined legislation infringes upon a fundamental right or discriminates against a discrete and insular minority, the exacting standard of strict scrutiny is triggered. To survive, the allegedly offensive legislation must be narrowly tailored to a compelling government interest. CHEMERINSKY, *supra* note 34, at 795.

42 Williamson, 348 U.S. 483.

43 508 U.S. 307, 313-15 (1993).

44 *Id.*

legislation has a "strong presumption of validity," and challengers of the legislation must "negative every conceivable basis which might support it."[45] Under such an inquiry, the legislature responsible for the regulation is not even required to articulate its reasons for enacting the law; a court may support a law by "rational speculation unsupported by evidence or empirical data."[46] Although professing to provide some measure of scrutiny, the rational basis test has been described as little more than a vehicle for judicial abdication of responsibility.[47] And while the test was spawned in contemplation of economic regulations,[48] its use would not be confined to the economic sphere.[49]

II. CERTAIN RIGHTS CANNOT BE NEATLY CABINED INTO ECONOMIC AND INDIVIDUAL CATEGORIES

Despite the best efforts of partisan factions, many asserted rights cannot be neatly cabined into economic or individual categories.[50] Moreover, in certain areas, the Court has flatly rejected this distinction, doing much to blur the lines between so-called individual and economic rights.[51] Campaign finance law, and its surrounding acrimony, provides a useful starting point for this discussion.

A. Campaign Finance Law

Freedom of speech is among the most highly revered guarantees of the Bill of Rights.[52] Within this domain, political speech is thought to be one of the most

---

[45] *Id.* at 314-15.

[46] *Id.*

[47] Clark Neily, *One Test, Two Standards: The On-And-Off Role Of "Plausibility" In Rational Basis Review*, 4 GEO. J. L. & PUB. POL'Y 199 (2006) (arguing that the rational basis test is the Supreme Court's junk drawer for disfavored constitutional rights that, while not explicitly repudiated, are not enforced in any meaningful way).

[48] As noted *supra*, *Carolene Products* is credited with the conception of the rational basis test while upholding the Filled Milk Act, a classic New Deal economic regulation. 304 U.S. 144 (1938).

[49] *See infra* Part III.

[50] *See infra* Part I.A-E.

[51] *See infra* Part I.D.

[52] *See e.g.*, Abrams v. United States, 250 U.S. 616, 630 (1919) (Holmes, J., dissenting) (commenting that "the ultimate good desired is better reached by free trade in ideas" and that "the best test of truth is the power of the thought to get itself accepted in the competition of the market"); Palko v. Connecticut, 302 U.S. 319, 327 (1937) (characterizing the First Amendment as "the matrix, the indispensable condition, of nearly every other form of freedom"); Frank S. Sengstock, *Achieving a Workable Definition of Free Speech: A Symposium on the Nature and Scope of the Constitutional Guarantee of Freedom of Expression*, 47 J. URB. L. 395, 396 (1970) (stating simply that "freedom of speech is essential to democracy"). Indeed, even the placement of free speech protection within the very first amendment to the Constitution suggests its value.

evolved forms of expression.[53] According to the Supreme Court, "the First Amendment has its 'fullest and most urgent application' to speech uttered during a campaign for political office."[54] Equally firm is our resolve to rid the electoral process of the corrupting influence of financial interests.[55] Campaign finance regulation represents the point of intersection between these two, sometimes competing policies.[56]

In campaign finance law, the debate is commonly concerned with whether financial contributions to campaigns for public office constitute an expression of protected political speech.[57] Decidedly not, argue proponents of campaign finance laws, who tout regulation of contributions as a necessary prophylactic from the "political potentialities of wealth."[58] In contrast, critics of campaign finance regulation argue that, in a world where political speech is expensive, restricting the ability to fundraise for political advertising is tantamount to restricting the message itself.[59] As a matter of instinct, adherents to the

53 *See, e.g.*, Buckley v. Valeo, 424 U.S. 1, 14 (1976) ("[T]he First Amendment affords the broadest protection to [] political expression in order 'to assure (the) unfettered interchange of ideas for the bringing about of political and social changes desired by the people.'") (citing Roth v. United States, 354 U.S. 476, 484 (1957)); Red Lion Broadcasting Co. v. FCC, 395 U.S. 367, 390 (1969) ("Speech concerning public affairs is more than self-expression; it is the essence of self-government.") (citing Garrison v. Louisiana, 379 U.S. 64, 74-75 (1964)); Mills v. Alabama, 384 U.S. 214, 218 (1966) ("[A] major purpose of [the First] Amendment was to protect the free discussion of governmental affairs.").

54 Eu v. S.F. County Democratic Central Comm., 489 U.S. 214, 223 (1989) (quoting Monitor Patriot Co. v. Roy, 401 U.S. 265, 272 (1971)).

55 *See, e.g.*, Fred Wertheimer & Susan Weiss Manes, *Campaign Finance Reform: A Key to Restoring the Health of Our Democracy*, *in* THE CONSTITUTION AND CAMPAIGN FINANCE REFORM, AN ANTHOLOGY 158 (2d. ed., Frederick G. Slabach ed., 2006).

56 *Id.*

57 *Compare* J. Skelly Wright, *Politics and the Constitution: Is Money Speech?*, *in* THE CONSTITUTION AND CAMPAIGN FINANCE REFORM, AN ANTHOLOGY (2d. ed., Frederick G. Slabach ed., 2006) (arguing that the view that campaign monies are tantamount to speech is a misconception of the First Amendment because it fails to embrace a community process whereby politicians prevail based on their worth, not based on their warchests), *with* Lillian R. BeVier, *Money and Politics: A Perspective on the First Amendment and Campaign Finance Reform*, *in* THE CONSTITUTION AND CAMPAIGN FINANCE REFORM, AN ANTHOLOGY 147 (2d. ed., Frederick G. Slabach ed., 2006) ("Not only does money permit the purchase of communication, but . . . political giving and spending are themselves communicative acts.").

58 McConnell v. Federal Election Com'n, 540 U.S. 93, 116 (2003). *See also*, 2 Rodney A. Smolla, SMOLLA AND NIMMER ON FREEDOM OF SPEECH, 16-16 (2006) ("Expenditure limits attempt to curb the political market power of the wealthy, serving the egalitarian goal of leveling the influence of various individuals among the populace – a sort of 'one person, one dollar, one vote' ideal.").

59 *See, e.g.*, Floyd Abrams, *Campaign Finance Restrictions Violate the Constitution*, Wall St. J., Apr. 9, 1998, at A22; Edward Crane, *Hard Boot for Soft Money?*, N.Y. Daily News, Sept. 30, 1997; Lillian

individual/economic rights dichotomy may side with the former clique in arguing that money bears no relation to speech. In *Buckley v. Valeo*,[60] however, the Supreme Court rejected this very notion.[61] In a per curiam decision, 150 pages in length, the Court held that certain campaign expenditures are, in fact, a protected form of expression.[62] The length and complexity of the decision alone suggest the difficulty of the issue presented.[63]

The *Buckley* Court considered a challenge to the 1974 amendments to the Federal Election Campaign Act of 1971 ("FECA").[64] The portions of the amendments most relevant to this Article imposed limits on both direct contributions to candidates and independent expenditures by individuals and groups "relative to a clearly identified candidate."[65] The Court of Appeals for the District of Columbia Circuit upheld the Act's limits on contributions and independent expenditures on the grounds that they should properly be regarded as regulating conduct, not speech.[66] Thus, to some degree, the Court of Appeals seems to have sided with those who insist that financial contributions are distinct from speech. The Supreme Court, however, expressly rejected this view and instead acknowledged that

> [a] restriction on the amount of money a person or group can spend on political communication during a campaign necessarily reduces the quantity of expression by restricting the number of issues discussed, the depth of their exploration, and the size of the audience reached. This is because virtually every means of

R. BeVier, *Campaign Finance "Reform" Proposals: A First Amendment Analysis*, CATO INST. POL'Y ANALYSIS No. 282, Sept. 4, 1997.

60 424 U.S. 1 (1976).

61 *Id.* at 19.

62 *Id.* at 45.

63 Similarly, a more recent Supreme Court case to consider campaign finance laws, McConnell v. Fed. Election Comm'n, resulted in a lengthy, 300 page, 5-4 decision. 540 U.S. 93 (2003).

64 Buckley, 424 U.S. at 6. These amendments, adopted in the wake of the Watergate scandal, sought to curb what was seen as the harmful effects of financial contributions on the election process. 2 U.S.C. § 441; Final Report S. Senate, S. Rep. No. 93-981, 93d Cong., 2d Sess. (1974).

65 424 U.S. at 7. The amendments also limited expenditures by a candidate, created disclosure requirements, established public funding for presidential elections, and established the Federal Elections Committee. *Id.*

66 *Id.* at 15-16; Buckley v. Valeo, 519 F.2d 821 (D.C. Cir 1975). In reaching this conclusion, the Court of Appeals relied upon *United States v. O'Brien*, 391 U.S. 367 (1968), which formulated a test for evaluating restrictions on conduct that accompanied speech, but was not itself pure speech. 424 U.S. 15-16.

> communicating ideas in today's mass society requires the expenditure of money.[67]

Notably, the Court observed that "[b]eing free to engage in unlimited political expression subject to a ceiling on expenditures is like being free to drive an automobile as far and as often as one desires on a single tank of gasoline."[68] Thus, the Court struck down the provisions of FECA restricting independent expenditures by individuals and groups on behalf of candidates.[69] In so doing, the Court recognized that freedom of speech in the political arena is contingent, to some degree, upon having the liberty to purchase the means of communication – a decidedly economic affair.[70]

This relation of money to speech would seem to confound the strictest iterations of the individual/economic rights dichotomy; the Court has essentially declared that certain economic activities are protected as political speech.[71] But the Court did not fully commit to this position. Although it struck down the restrictions on independent expenditures on behalf of candidates, the Court upheld limitations on individual or group contributions directly to a specific candidate.[72] This distinction is highly criticized[73] and

---

67 424 U.S. at 19.

68 *Id.* at 19, n.18.

69 424 U.S. at 48-49.

70 *See*, Lillian R. BeVier, *Campaign Finance Reform: Specious Arguments, Intractable Dilemmas*, 94 COLUM. L. REV. 1258, 1277 (1994).

71 *Id.* at 15-23, 39; The Court explained:

> The Act's expenditure ceilings impose direct and substantial restraints on the quantity of political speech . . . . It is clear that a primary effect of these expenditure limitations is to restrict the quantity of campaign speech by individuals, groups, and candidates. The restrictions, while neutral as to the ideas expressed, limit political expression "at the core of our electoral process and of the First Amendment freedoms."

Id. (quoting Williams v. Rhodes, 393 U.S. 23, 32 (1968)).

72 *Id.* at 29. The *Buckley* Court asserted that limits on such contributions impose "only a marginal restriction" on free speech and that a "contribution serves as a general expression of support for the candidate and his views, but does not communicate the underlying basis for the support." *Id.* at 20-21. Thus, contributions by individuals directly to a candidate for Senate may be limited, but the same individual's own purchase of a full page newspaper advertisement on behalf of that candidate may not.

73 *See, e.g.*, Jamin B. Raskin & John Bonifaz, *The Constitutional Imperative and Practical Superiority of Democratically Financed Elections*, 94 COLUM. L. REV. 1160 (1994). Justice Thomas commented, "I would reject the framework established by *Buckley v. Valeo* . . . . Instead, I begin with the premise that there is no constitutionally significant difference between campaign contributions

perhaps a product of the inherent difficulty of distinguishing economic and noneconomic activities. Certainly, even those who insist that individual and economic rights are categorically distinct must agree that the exercise of political speech often depends on having some measure of economic liberty, be it purchasing network airtime, printing pamphlets, or even buying a soapbox on which to stand.[74] Although the Court stopped short of a full proclamation that money is speech, at a minimum, *Buckley* leaves us with the assertion that some financial expenditures are tantamount to speech and warrant protection as such.[75]

The Washington State Supreme Court recently decided a campaign finance case that uniquely illustrates the difficulty in distinguishing economic contributions from protected speech.[76] Kirby Wilbur and John Carlson, two radio personalities on KVI 570 AM in Seattle, Washington, promoted a ballot initiative on-air that would roll back a recent gas tax increase.[77] Local prosecutors brought a complaint against the sponsors of the ballot initiative, alleging that the on-air promotion by Wilbur and Carlson constituted an in-kind contribution.[78] The Thurston County Superior Court agreed and issued a preliminary injunction, ordering the campaign to disclose the on-air discussions as in-kind contributions.[79] Notably, Washington law prohibits contributions to initiative campaigns in excess of $5,000 within 21 days of a general election.[80]

---

and expenditures: both forms of speech are central to the First Amendment." Colo. Republican Fed. Campaign Comm. v. Fed. Election Comm'n, 518 U.S. 604, 631, 640 (1996) (Thomas, J., concurring in part, dissenting in part).

74 BeVier, *Money and Politics*, *supra* note 57, at 147 (succinctly noting that "money permit[s] the purchase of communication.").

75 *See* BeVier, *supra* note 70. *But see* J. Skelly Wright, *Politics and the Constitution: Is Money Speech?*, 85 YALE L. J. 1001 (1976).

76 San Juan County v. No New Gas Tax, No. 77966-0, 2007 Wash. LEXIS 297 (Wash. Apr. 26, 2007).

77 Senate Bill 6103 increased the state's gasoline tax by 9.5 cents per gallon over four years. The internet incarnation of this campaign was nonewgastax.com.

78 San Juan County v. No New Gas Tax, No. 05-2-01205-3, slip op. at 1-2 (Thurston County Super. Ct. Oct. 25, 2005). An in-kind contribution is a non-monetary donation, such as printing services or telephone equipment, which can be given a cash value. *Id.*

79 San Juan County v. No New Gas Tax, No. 05-2-01205-3, slip op. at 1-2 (Thurston County Super. Ct. July 1, 2005) (Order Granting Preliminary Injunction Requiring compliance With Fair Campaign Practices Act).

80 RCW 42.17.105(8). This section of the statute states:

> It is a violation of this chapter for any person to make, or for any candidate or political committee to accept from any one person, contributions reportable under RCW 42.17.090 in the aggregate exceeding fifty thousand dollars for any campaign for statewide office or exceeding five thousand dollars for any other campaign subject to the provisions of this chapter within twenty-one days of a general election. This

Thus, if an on-air discussion is valued at over $5,000, campaign finance regulations could literally be used to silence political speech. The Washington Supreme Court reversed the lower court's ruling,[81] but the implication remains clear: money and speech are not always easily divorced.

Certainly, the commodification of speech in any form offends the individual/economic rights dichotomy, which would suggest that speech is inherently distinct from money and cannot be reduced to mere financial value. By assigning a dollar amount to Wilbur and Carlson's on-air speech, the Thurston County Superior Court illustrated the point that money is simply a medium of exchange and may represent other goods or forms of expression. Ironically, it is under the same framework of campaign finance law supported by those who argue that money is distinct from speech that speech has been equated to money. Whether one agrees with the *Buckley* Court or the Thurston County Superior Court, both decisions complicate purist views of the individual/economic rights dichotomy. Likewise, both provide compelling authority for a less dogmatic approach to distinguishing rights along economic or noneconomic lines.

B. *Commercial Speech*

In similar fashion, the jurisprudence of commercial speech further complicates the individual/economic rights dichotomy. At the heart of this issue, some argue that speech should be afforded less protection when tainted with the indicia of commerce.[82] Commercial speech, according to this argument, does nothing to serve the objectives of the First Amendment, namely, promoting self-government by increasing participation in the political process.[83] Others

---

subsection does not apply to contributions made by, or accepted from, a bona fide political party as defined in this chapter, excluding the county central committee or legislative district committee.

Id.

81 San Juan County v. No New Gas Tax, No. 77966-0, 2007 Wash. LEXIS 297 (Wash. Apr. 26, 2007).

82 *See, e.g.*, Thomas Jackson & John Jeffries, Jr., *Commercial Speech: Economic Due Process and The First Amendment*, 65 VA. L. REV. 1 (1979); Lillian BeVier, *The First Amendment and Political Speech: An Inquiry Into the Substance and Limits of Principle*, 30 STAN. L. REV. 299 (1978) (arguing against constitutional protection for commercial speech as it promotes neither the political process nor public decision making).

83 Jackson & Jeffries, *supra* note 82, at 5-6 ("The first amendment guarantee of freedom of speech and press protects only certain identifiable values. Chief among them is effective self-government. Additionally, the first amendment may protect the opportunity for individual self-fulfillment through free expression. Neither value is implicated by governmental regulation of

argue that commercial speech provides important information to consumers and is indistinguishable from other forms of speech.[84] Sadly, the Court's many attempts at settling this issue have left more questions than answers.[85]

Initially, in *Valentine v. Chrestensen*,[86] the Court experimented with the notion that the First Amendment provided no protection for commercial speech. Over a First Amendment challenge, the Court upheld a New York City ordinance that singled out commercial speech by prohibiting the distribution of any "handbill . . . or other advertising matter in or upon any street or public place."[87] F.J. Chrestensen was advised by the Police Commissioner that he could not distribute handbills advertising the exhibition of a former U.S. Navy submarine that he owned.[88] Under this ordinance, however, handbills devoted to "information or a public protest" were allowed.[89] Perhaps befuddled by this confounded distinction, Chrestensen reprinted the handbills.[90] On one side was the original advertisement minus the mention of an admission fee, and on the other side was a protest against the City Dock Department for refusing him wharfage facilities.[91] Chrestensen was detained for distributing the new double-sided handbills, and he sought an injunction against enforcement of the ordinance.[92] The District Court granted his injunction, invalidating the ordinance,[93] and the Circuit Court of Appeals affirmed.[94] Nonetheless, Justice

commercial speech."); BeVier, *supra* note 82, at 358 ("The sole legitimate first amendment principle protects only speech that participates in the process of representative democracy.")

84 *See, e.g.*, Steven Shiffrin, *The First Amendment and Economic Regulation: Away From a General Theory of the First Amendment*, 78 NW. U. L. REV. 1212, 1222-35 (1983) (arguing that commercial speech is difficult to separate from political speech); Rodney A. Smolla, *Information, Imagery, and the First Amendment: A Case for Expansive Protection of Commercial Speech*, 71 TEX. L. REV. 777, 780-81 (1993) (arguing that commercial speech should have a presumption of protection because there is no convincing argument for its exclusion and because "[i]t is only the linkage between commercial speech and a commercial transaction that gives government the theoretical leverage to presume to regulate the speech at all."). Smolla also argues that Supreme Court case law suggests that the mere motive of profit is not enough to disqualify commercial speech from full First Amendment protection. *Id.* at 781-82.

85 Vincent Blasi, *The Pathological Perspective and the First Amendment*, 85 COLUM. L. REV. 449, 486 (1985); C. Edwin Baker, *Commercial Speech: A Problem in the Theory of Freedom*, 62 IOWA L. REV. 1 (1976).

86 316 U.S. 52 (1942).

87 *Id.* at 53.

88 316 U.S. at 52-53.

89 *Id.* at 53, n.1.

90 *Id.* at 53.

91 *Id.* at 53.

92 *Id.* at 53-54.

93 Chrestensen v. Valentine, 34 F. Supp. 596 (S.D.N.Y. 1940).

94 Chrestensen v. Valentine, 122 F.2d 511 (2d Cir. 1941).

Roberts declared, with neither analysis nor explanation, that "[w]e are [] clear that the Constitution imposes no such restraint on government as respects purely commercial advertising."[95] Thus, in bold strokes, Justice Roberts upheld the individual/economic rights distinction.

Commercial speech remained unprotected until 1975, when the Court reconsidered this position. In *Bigelow v. Virginia*, the Court struck down a state law that made it a crime to "encourage or promote" abortions "by the sale or circulation of any publication."[96] Jeffrey Cole Bigelow had been convicted under this statute for running an advertisement in his newspaper, The *Virginia Weekly*, which indicated the availability of low-cost abortions in New York.[97] The Supreme Court of Virginia upheld Bigelow's conviction on the assumption that the First Amendment did not protect commercial speech,[98] but Justice Blackmun reversed, expressly holding that "speech is not stripped of First Amendment protection merely because it appears" in commercial form.[99] The Court further declared that "[t]he fact that the particular advertisement in appellant's newspaper had commercial aspects or reflected the advertiser's commercial interests did not negate all First Amendment guarantees."[100]

A year later, in *Virginia Pharmacy*,[101] the Court reaffirmed the notion that commercial speech was protected by the First Amendment. Here, the Court struck down a Virginia state law that prohibited advertising the price of prescription drugs.[102] Justice Blackmun again declared that speech that "does no more than propose a commercial transaction" is protected by the First Amendment.[103] Observing that the interests of contestants in a labor dispute are no less economic, the Court declared that the motives of the speaker should

---

95 Chrestensen, 316 U.S. at 54.

96 421 U.S. 809, 813 n.3 (1975); VA. CODE ANN. § 18.1-63 (1960) ("If any person, by publication, lecture, advertisement, or by the sale or circulation of any publication, or in any other manner, encourage or prompt the procuring of abortion or miscarriage, he shall be guilty of a misdemeanor."). The Court noted that the statute dated back to 1878, but that "Bigelow's was the first prosecution under the statute 'in modern times,' and perhaps the only prosecution under it 'at any time.'" 421 U.S. at 813 n.2 (citing Transcript of Oral Arguments, 40).

97 *Id.* at 811.

98 *Id.* at 818.

99 *Id.*

100 412 U.S. at 818.

101 Virginia State Board of Pharmacy v. Virginia Citizens Consumer Council Inc., 425 U.S. 748 (1976).

102 *Id.* at 749 (quoting VA. CODE ANN. § 54-524.35 (1974) ("a pharmacist licensed in Virginia is guilty of unprofessional conduct if he '(3) publishes, advertises or promotes, directly or indirectly, in any manner whatsoever, any amount, price, fee, premium, discount, rebate or credit terms... for any drugs which may be dispensed only by prescription.'").

103 *Id.* at 762.

not determine the level of protection afforded to the speech.[104] The opinion practically reveres commercial speech.

> As to the particular consumer's interest in the free flow of commercial information, that interest may be as keen, if not keener by far, than his interest in the day's most urgent political debate. . . . When drug prices vary as strikingly as they do, information as to who is charging what becomes more than a convenience. It could mean the alleviation of physical pain or the enjoyment of basic necessities.[105]

To this day, commercial speech is afforded constitutional protection, but it is not on par with the level of protection afforded noncommercial speech.[106] On this issue, the Court seems to adhere to some degree to the

---

104 *Id.* at 762-63.

105 *Id.* at 763-64. In *Virginia Pharmacy*, Justice Blackmun even addressed and rejected the argument that commercial speech does not contribute to the self-government rationale for the First Amendment:

> Moreover, there is another consideration that suggests that no line between publicly "interesting" or "important" commercial advertising and the opposite kind could ever be drawn. Advertising, however tasteless and excessive it sometimes may seem, is nonetheless dissemination of information as to who is producing and selling what product, for what reason, and at what price. So long as we preserve a predominantly free enterprise economy, the allocation of our resources in large measure will be made through numerous private economic decisions. It is a matter of public interest that those decisions, in the aggregate, be intelligent and well informed. To this end, the free flow of commercial information is indispensable. . . . And if it is indispensable to the proper allocation of resources in a free enterprise system, it is also indispensable to the formation of intelligent opinions as to how that system ought to be regulated or altered. Therefore, even if the First Amendment were thought to be primarily an instrument to enlighten public decisionmaking in a democracy, we could not say that the free flow of information does not serve that goal.

429 U.S. at 765.

106 Unlike its noncommercial counterpart, commercial speech involving illegal activity or false and misleading expressions does not enjoy First Amendment protections. Pittsburgh Press Co. v. Pittsburgh Commission on Human Relations, 413 U.S. 376 (1973) (upholding a ban on advertising an illegal product, viz., gender-specific employment); Friedman v. Rogers, 440 U.S. 1 (1979) (upholding regulation of the use of trade names in commercial advertising). Also, the overbreadth doctrine does not apply to commercial speech. Bates v. State Bar of Arizona, 433 U.S. 350 (1977). Commercial speech is also analyzed under a less searching standard of review than is noncommercial speech. Central Hudson Gas & Electric Corp. v. Public Service Comm'n, 447 U.S. 557 (1980).

individual/economic rights distinction. Nonetheless, the Court has never offered a convincing explanation of why commercial speech is subject to less protection.[107]

The *Central Hudson* Court articulated an intricate four-part test for evaluating the constitutionality of commercial speech regulation,[108] but offered little in the way of justifying this distinction. Speaking through Justice Powell, the Court purportedly "recognized 'the commonsense distinction between speech proposing a commercial transaction, which occurs in an area traditionally subject to governmental regulation, and other varieties of speech.'"[109] Justice Powell concluded, "[t]he Constitution therefore accords a lesser protection to commercial speech than to other constitutionally guaranteed expression."[110] But this justification does little more than declare that commercial speech warrants less protection because it occurs in a commercial zone. Such tautology does little to explain the Court's disparate treatment of commercial and noncommercial speech.[111]

In addition to the debate over whether or why commercial speech should be protected is the question of how to define commercial speech. Obviously, advertising product pricing information is commercial speech.[112] But the definition of commercial speech as "advertising" is at the same time too broad and too narrow.[113] This definition would include some forms of pure political speech, such as the "editorial advertisement"[114] protesting the treatment of civil rights leaders that was the basis for *New York Times v. Sullivan*.[115] But this definition would not include commercial speech other than advertising, such as

---

107 Smolla, *supra* note 84, at 780 ("In my view, there are no convincing arguments for disqualifying most modern mass advertising from constitutional protection.").

108 447 U.S. at 566.

109 Central Hudson, 447 U.S. at 562.

110 447 U.S. at 563.

111 *See* Smolla, *supra* note 84, at 780. Also, singling out commercial speech by affording it a lesser degree of protection seems to violate the prime directive of First Amendment theory, that content-based distinctions are presumptively unconstitutional. *See, e.g.*, Texas v. Johnson, 491 U.S. 397, 414 (1989) ("If there is a bedrock principle underlying the First Amendment, it is that the government may not prohibit the expression of an idea simply because society finds the idea itself offensive or disagreeable."); Members of City Council v. Taxpayers for Vincent, 466 U.S. 789, 804 (1984) ("the First Amendment forbids the government to regulate speech in ways that favor some viewpoints or ideas at the expense of others.").

112 CHEMERINSKY, *infra* note 34, at 1088.

113 *Id.*

114 New York Times v. Sullivan, 376 U.S. 254, 266 (1964) (reversing judgment for plaintiff in civil libel act and establishing the "actual malice" standard for defamation and libel.).

115 *Id.* at 256.

a lobbyist's communiqué to a government official or a corporate financial statement issued to a stockholder.[116]

In *Central Hudson*,[117] the Court defined commercial speech as "expression related solely to the economic interests of the speaker and its audience."[118] This definition, however, also has its shortcomings.[119] A newspaper publisher or a business school professor may have purely economic motives for printing papers or lecturing, just as the reader or student may have the same economic motives for reading the paper or listening to the lectures.[120] Nonetheless, these forms of expression cannot rightly be considered commercial.

In *Bolger v. Youngs Drug Products Corp.*,[121] the Court directly addressed the issue of what constitutes commercial speech. Youngs, the manufacturer of Trojan brand condoms, was distributing flyers and pamphlets with such titles as "Condoms and Human Sexuality" and "Plain Talk about Venereal Disease," which discussed both prophylactics in general and particular products of Youngs.'[122] In an attempt to describe commercial speech, the Court stated:

> The mere fact that these pamphlets are conceded to be advertisements clearly does not compel the conclusion that they are commercial speech. Similarly, the reference to a specific product does not by itself render the pamphlets commercial speech. Finally, the fact that Youngs has an economic motivation for mailing the pamphlets would clearly be insufficient by itself to turn the materials into commercial speech. The combination of *all* these characteristics, however, provides strong support for the District Court's conclusion that the informational pamphlets are properly characterized as commercial speech.[123]

Thus, according to the Court, commercial speech has three characteristics: (1) it is an advertisement, (2) referring to specific products, and (3) is economically motivated.[124] However well-articulated this test may be, it is no conclusive

[116] *See* CHEMERINSKY, *infra* note 34, at 1088.
[117] 447 U.S. 557 (1980).
[118] Central Hudson, 447 U.S. at 561.
[119] CHEMERINSKY, *infra* note 34, at 1088.
[120] *See id.*
[121] 463 U.S. 60 (1983).
[122] *Id.* at 62.
[123] *Id.* at 67 (citations omitted; emphasis in original).
[124] *Id.*

definition.[125] In the Court's own words, it merely "provides strong support" for a finding of commercial speech.[126] Furthermore, this description fails to capture as commercial speech advertisements promoting the image of a brand rather than a specific product.[127]

Truthfully, the distinction between commercial speech and "pure" speech cannot easily be drawn; speech is not always identifiable as commercial or noncommercial.[128] As the Honorable Loren A. Smith has observed, "[a] political commercial is hardly different in length, mass, chemical composition, or albedo than one for Pepsi or Marlboro."[129] Likewise, a picket organized by a labor union aims to influence consumer choice among available goods but is not typically considered commercial speech. As the Court's numerous false starts indicate, attempts to distinguish commercial from political speech are futile.[130] Indeed, considering the myriad financial rewards available to holders of public office, a candidate's motives for running for political office may consist largely of economic concerns. Does a certain composition of economic interest color speech commercial? If so, what level of economic interest is appropriate and, more importantly, how is a court to measure this interest?

Furthermore, despite its disfavored status, commercial speech may, nonetheless, provide some measure of political value.[131] An independent merchant advertising his outlet as an alternative to big box retailers may allow the listener to make both an economic and political choice. More over, the ability to advertise profit-making products has been the engine of the free press.[132] Without revenues from advertising, countless print, broadcast, and online media would struggle to stay in business, let alone provide quality content, including political coverage, to the masses. At a minimum, the difficulty in distinguishing between commercial speech and noncommercial

---

125 *See* Shiffrin, *supra* note 84, at 1223.
126 463 U.S. at 67.
127 *See* Laura Lin, Note, *Corporate Image Advertising and the First Amendment*, 61 S. CAL. L. REV. 459 (1988).
128 Ronald K.L. Collins & David M. Skover, THE DEATH OF DISCOURSE 70 (2d ed. 2005) (arguing that "public expression cannot be significantly separated from the influences of commercialism.").
129 Hon. Loren A. Smith, *Life, Liberty & Whose Property?: An Essay on Prop Rights*, 30 U. RICH. L. REV. 1055 (1996).
130 Shiffrin, *supra* note 84, at 1223.
131 Bruce M. Owen, ECONOMICS AND FREEDOM OF EXPRESSION, MEDIA STRUCTURE AND THE FIRST AMENDMENT 29 (1975).
132 *Id.* ("Thus 'popular' (economically viable) editorial content is sometimes produced in order to facilitate the consumption of advertising, as in sugar coating a pill.").

speech is emblematic of the larger difficulty of compartmentalizing rights into individual and economic spheres.[133]

C. Takings

In the context of takings, the Court has flatly rejected the individual/economic rights distinction.[134] Subscribers to the rights dichotomy would likely argue that a place of residence warrants greater privacy protection than does a place of business, which is already subject to myriad other regulations.[135] In *Dolan v. City of Tigard*,[136] the Court considered this very issue. After being denied a variance from the City's grant of a conditional construction permit,[137] Florance Dolan claimed that the City's actions violated the Fifth Amendment as a taking without just compensation. Despite the City's pleas that Dolan's property was a business and, thus, subject to less protection, the Court sided with Dolan.

Justice Stevens' dissent argued that economic rights are distinguishable from noneconomic rights in the takings context;[138] he would have dismissed the claim, finding the permit condition a mere "business regulation."[139] But in his majority opinion, Chief Justice Rehnquist rejected this argument, declaring that "[w]e see no reason why the Takings Clause of the Fifth Amendment, as much a part of the Bill of Rights as the First Amendment or Fourth Amendment, should be relegated to the status of a poor relation"[140] when applied to property being used for a business. Thus, the Court declined to adopt a different standard of deference when considering takings of commercial versus

---

133 *See infra* Part IV.

134 *See infra* note 139 and accompanying text.

135 *See. e.g.*, Johnston, *Constitutionality of Subdivision Control Exactions: The Quest for A Rationale*, 52 CORNELL L. Q. 871, 923 (1967).

> The subdivider is a manufacturer, processer, and marketer of a product; land is but one of his raw materials. In subdivision control disputes, the developer is not defending hearth and home against the king's intrusion, but simply attempting to maximize his profits from the sale of a finished product. As applied to him, subdivision control exactions are actually business regulations.

Id.

136 512 U.S. 374 (1994).

137 *Id.* at 377. Florance Dolan, an owner of a plumbing store, brought a challenge to the comprehensive land use plans of Tigard, Oregon. *Id.* After applying for a permit to expand the size of her store and pave a parking lot, the City granted her permit application, subject to the condition that she dedicate ten percent of her property for a bike path and greenway to alleviate congestion and flood water runoff from the pavement. *Id.* at 381.

138 *Id.* at 402 (Stevens, J., dissenting).

139 *Id.*

140 512 U.S. at 392.

noncommercial property. In this instance, the Court has rejected the distinction, if any, between individual and economic rights.

D. Congressional Legislation Under the Commerce Clause

In passing legislation under the Commerce Clause, Congress itself has provided many instances that blur the line between economic and noneconomic rights. Congress, no doubt, has the power to regulate interstate commerce.[141] On this one point, all serious theories of constitutional interpretation agree. What constitutes interstate commerce, however, has changed over time and is still a point of contentious debate. When the original Constitution was ratified, "commerce" consisted of "selling, buying, and bartering, as well as transporting for these purposes."[142] Thus, under this originalist view, Congress' ability to regulate interstate commerce would not reach activities such as manufacturing[143] or agriculture.[144]

While offering various tests for evaluating legislation passed under the Commerce Clause, the modern Court has provided little consistency in defining what constitutes a commercial action.[145] In *United States v. Lopez*, the Court recognized that, under the Commerce Clause, Congress may regulate three categories of activity, the "channels of interstate commerce," the "instrumentalities of interstate commerce," and "activities having a substantial relation to interstate commerce."[146] But each category depends upon some measure of tautology, simply rehashing the word "commerce."[147] Later in the

---

141 U.S. CONST. art. I, § 8, cl. 3. ("The Congress shall have power . . . [t]o regulate Commerce with foreign Nations, and among the several States, and with the Indian Tribes.")

142 United States v. Lopez, 514 U.S. 549, 585-86 (1995) (Thomas, J., concurring). *See also*, Compare Randy E. Barnett, *The Original Meaning of the Commerce Clause*, 68 U. CHI. L. REV. 101 (2001) (supporting Justice Thomas' view of commerce as selling, buying, and bartering and transporting for those purposes). *But see*, Grant S. Nelson and Robert J. Pushaw, Jr., *Rethinking the Commerce Clause: Applying First Principles to Uphold Federal Commercial Regulations but Preserve State Control over Social Issues*, 85 IOWA L. REV. 1, 13-20 (1999) (arguing that commerce originally referred to any gainful activity).

143 *See, e.g.*, United States v. E.C. Knight, 156 U.S. 1 (1895) (distinguishing commerce from manufacturing and agriculture).

144 *Id.*

145 *Compare* United States v. Lopez, 115 S. Ct. 1624, 1643 (1995) (suggesting that commerce denotes "sale and/or transport rather than business generally") (Thomas, J., concurring), *and* Kidd v. Pearson, 128 U.S. 1, 20 (1888) ("The buying and selling and the transportation incidental thereto constitute commerce"), *with* NLRB v. Jones & Laughlin Steel Corp., 301 U.S. 1, 31 (1936) ("The term 'commerce' means trade, traffic, commerce, transportation, or communication"), *and* Gibbons v. Ogden, 22 U.S. 1, (1824) (defining commerce as "intercourse").

146 *Id.* at 558-59.

147 514 U.S. 549, 558 (1995).

opinion, Chief Justice Rehnquist refers to an "economic enterprise" but offers no further definition of this amorphous term.[148] Does the mere involvement of money make an act commercial? Is bartering a commercial action? Does a trophy wife engage in an "economic enterprise?" Is it the motive of the actor, the character of the act, or the environment in which the act takes place that determines its status as commercial or noncommercial?

Whatever the definition of a commercial act, adherents of the rights dichotomy would anticipate Commerce Clause legislation to be focused on common sense notions of commercial actions. However, much legislation passed under the broad auspices of the Commerce Clause has been aimed at decidedly noncommercial behavior, instead implicating rights of a more individual nature.[149] Touching on issues such as gambling, prostitution, drug use, and even consensual sex between partners, the following decisions reflect a nexus between economic and noneconomic interests propounded by both the Court and Congress.

1. The Lottery Case

In the nineteenth century, the federal government had no power to police public health, safety, and morals.[150] Rather, this domain was exclusively reserved to the states.[151] Nonetheless, in the early twentieth century, Congress

---

148 *Id.* at 561.

149 *See infra* Part III.E.1-2; Robert J. Steamer, *Commerce Power*, in THE OXFORD COMPANION TO THE SUPREME COURT OF THE UNITED STATES 168 (Kermit L. Hall et al. eds., 1992) (explaining Congress' indirect regulation of the public health, morals, safety, and welfare under the Commerce Clause).

150 Under the Constitution, Congress has explicit power to criminalize only counterfeiting, "Piracies and Felonies committed on the high Seas, and Offences against the Law of Nations," offenses committed on federal property, see *Id.* at cl. 17; and treason. U.S. CONST. art. I, 8, cl. 6, 10, 17; *Id.* at art. III, 3, cl. 2. Although the First Congress soon criminalized other conduct, such as obstruction of justice in federal courts, see Crimes Act of 1790, 1 Stat. 112, until the Reconstruction era, federal criminal law was limited to "punishment of acts directly injurious to the central government." L.B. Schwartz, *Federal Criminal Jurisdiction and Prosecutors' Discretion*, 13 LAW & CONTEMP. PROBS. 64, 65 (1948). See also Dwight F. Henderson, CONGRESS, COURTS, AND CRIMINALS: THE DEVELOPMENT OF FEDERAL CRIMINAL LAW, 1801-1829 (1985). On this basis, Justice Thomas would question the legitimacy of the current federal police power doctrine. United States v. Lopez, 514 U.S. 549, 584-85 (1995) (Thomas, J., concurring) ("[t]he Federal Government has nothing approaching a police power.").

151 U.S. CONST. amend. X. ("The powers not delegated to the United States by the Constitution, nor prohibited by it to the States, are reserved to the States respectively, or to the people."). See also, United States v. E. C. Knight Co., 156 U.S. 1, 11 (1895).

> It cannot be denied that the power of a State to protect the lives, health, and property of its citizens, and to preserve good order and the public morals, "the

extracted unprecedented mileage out of the Commerce Clause, directly regulating the public's health and morals.[152] In 1895, under its authority to regulate commerce, Congress passed the Lottery Act,[153] which prohibited transporting tickets offering "prizes dependent upon lot or chance" from one state to another.[154] In *Champion v. Ames*,[155] the Court considered the constitutionality of this Act.

Depending upon how the debate is framed, the Lottery Act could be seen as the regulation of economic or noneconomic actions. Some may argue that the Lottery Act restricted the operations of a shipping business, or even the end user's ability to spend, and occasionally win, money on games of chance. On the other hand, some may argue that the Act regulates an immoral individual action – gambling. As the Lottery Act was passed under the Commerce Clause, one would expect its proponents to champion the former view, noting the presence of money. The Court, however, upheld the Lottery Act for an admittedly noneconomic purpose: eradicating the "widespread pestilence of lotteries."[156]

Rather than arguing that the conduct in question was indeed commerce, and that the regulation of this commerce was proper, the Court boldly asserted that the federal government, similar to the states, had the power to regulate elements "injurious to the public morals."[157] Justice Harlan declared,

> [i]f a State, when considering legislation for the suppression of lotteries within its own limits, may properly take into view the evils that inhere in the raising of money, in that mode, why may not Congress, invested

---

> power to govern men and things within the limits of its dominion," is a power originally and always belonging to the States, not surrendered by them to the general government, nor directly restrained by the Constitution of the United States, and essentially exclusive.

Id.

152 Russell L. Weaver, *Federalism and the Criminal Justice System: Lopez and the Federalization Of Criminal Law*, 98 W. VA. L. REV. 815 (1996) (documenting early statutes in which Congress federalized many aspects of the criminal law).

153 28 U.S.C. § 963 (1895) (more formally known as "An Act for the Suppression of Lottery Traffic through National and Interstate Commerce and the Postal Service, Subject to the Jurisdiction and Laws of the United States").

154 *Id.*

155 Champion v. Ames, 188 U.S. 321 (1903). Charles Champion was convicted under the act and challenged it, insisting that carrying lottery tickets from one state to another did not constitute commerce within the meaning of the commerce clause. *Id.* at 322.

156 *Id.* at 356.

157 *Id.* at 357.

> with power to regulate commerce among the several States, provide that such commerce shall not be polluted by the carrying of lottery tickets from one State to another? In this connection it must not be forgotten that the power of Congress to regulate commerce among the states is plenary, is complete in itself, and is subject to no limitations except such as may be found in the Constitution.[158]

With good reason, some may remain unconvinced that gambling is an individual act, rather than an economic act; gambling does usually involve transfers of wealth. But rather than addressing this issue, the Court, in broad strokes, asserted that Congress, under its power to regulate commerce, also had the power to regulate morality, a decidedly noneconomic sphere. Thus, even though it could be fairly argued that the Lottery Act affected economic behavior, the Court did not even bother professing it as such. Instead, the Court conflated the power to regulate commerce with the ability to regulate morality and, in so doing, rejected even a surface-level adherence to the view that economic rights are distinct from other interests.

2. The Mann Act

Another early example of the Commerce Clause being used to target primarily noncommercial behavior is the Mann Act, which prohibited transporting women across state lines for "immoral purposes."[159] In *Hoke v. United States*,[160] the Court considered the constitutionality of the Mann Act in the face of a claim that the Commerce Clause did not grant Congress the authority to regulate "prostitution or any other immorality of citizens of the several states . . . ."[161]

This debate should have centered on the legitimate question of whether prostitution is a form of commerce subject to regulation by Congress. Arguably, prostitution is an "economic endeavor;" prostitution, by definition,

---

[158] *Id.* at 356; In this decision, the Court also made clear that the power to regulate commerce included the power to prohibit it. *Id.* at 358-62.

[159] 36 Stat. 825, c. 395. The Mann Act was more formally known as "An Act to Further Regulate Interstate and Foreign Commerce by Prohibiting the Transportation Therein for Immoral Purposes of Women and Girls, and for Other Purposes." Notable persons prosecuted under the Mann Act include Chuck Berry, Charlie Chaplin, Rex Ingram, Jack Johnson, W. I. Thomas, and Frank Lloyd Wright.

[160] Hoke v. US, 227 U.S. 308 (1913).

[161] *Id.* at 319.

involves an exchange of money,[162] and some men and women certainly earn their living through such exchanges. But instead of even addressing this issue, the Court openly acknowledged that the purpose of the Act was to regulate morality where the states could not. Justice McKenna declared,

> There is unquestionably a control in the states over the morals of their citizens, and, it may be admitted, it extends to making prostitution a crime. It is a control, however, which can be exercised only within the jurisdiction of the states, but there is a domain which the states cannot reach and over which Congress alone has power; and if such power be exerted to control what the states cannot, it is an argument for--not against--its legality.[163]

And thus, the Court found the Mann Act valid, while admitting it had more to do with regulating morality than regulating economic activities. Although prostitution may arguably be an act of commerce, the Court declared that Congress' power to regulate commerce may be wielded toward a noncommercial end.[164] With this understanding of the Commerce Clause, the application of the Mann Act to noncommercial consensual extramarital sex is somewhat less difficult to swallow. In *Caminetti v. United States*,[165] the Court considered this very issue.

Caminetti was convicted under the Mann Act[166] and challenged its constitutionality, arguing that the Mann Act reached only "commercialized vice."[167] Again, instead of focusing on whether the conduct in question was of a commercial nature, Justice Day inquired into whether transporting a woman for the purpose of becoming a concubine was an "immoral practice"[168] within the plain meaning[169] of that term. Finding that it was,[170] the Court upheld the

---

162 BLACK'S LAW DICTIONARY (8th ed. 2004) (defining prostitution as "[t]he act or practice of engaging in sexual activity for money or its equivalent; commercialized sex.").

163 227 U.S. at 321.

164 *See id.*

165 Caminetti v. US, 242 U.S. 470 (1917); This case is a consolidation of three cases. For purposes of this paper, the central focus is on the Caminetti case.

166 Caminetti was convicted for transporting a woman from Sacramento, California, to Reno, Nevada, for the purpose of making her his "mistress and concubine." *Id.* at 483.

167 *Id.* at 484.

168 *Id.* at 486

169 This case is also notable as being one of the first to embrace the Plain Meaning Rule of statutory construction, whereby a court is encouraged to interpret and enforce an otherwise constitutional statute according to the ordinary meaning of the its language. *Id.* at 485.

170 Caminetti, 242 U.S. at 485.

Mann Act, as applied to noncommercial consensual extramarital sex, as a valid exercise of Congress' power to regulate commerce.[171]

For better or for worse, the power of Congress to "regulate commerce among the several states"[172] has reached spheres of human action that cannot rightly be considered commercial.[173] By extending the power to regulate commerce to include the regulation of individual morality, the Court and Congress have, to some extent, blurred the distinction between individual and economic rights.[174]

> To cause a woman or girl to be transported for the purposes of debauchery, and for an immoral purpose, to wit, becoming a concubine or mistress. . . would seem by the very statement of the facts to embrace transportation for purposes denounced by the act, and therefore fairly within its meaning. While such immoral purpose would be more culpable in morals and attributed to baser motives if accompanied with the expectation of pecuniary gain, such considerations do not prevent the lesser offense against morals of furnishing transportation in order that a woman may be debauched, or become a mistress or a concubine, from being the execution of purposes within the meaning of this law.

Id.

171 Polygamy was also found to be an "immoral purpose" under the Act in Cleveland v. US, 329 U.S. 14, 16-17 (1946).

172 U.S. CONST. art. I, § 8, cl. 3.

173 *See* Steamer, *supra* note 149.

174 Other legislative action has also blurred the line between individual and economic rights and warrants brief exploration. The 1996 Solomon Amendment, 10 U.S.C. § 983(b), allows Congress to withhold federal grants from an institution of higher education if it denies equal campus access to military recruiters. Conditional spending is certainly an economic activity, but this issue, nonetheless, implicates an individual right, free association. Rumsfield v. Forum for Academic & Institutional Rights, 547 U.S. ___, 126 S. Ct. 1297 (2006), recently upheld the Solomon Amendment as a valid exercise of Congress' power under the Spending Clause. In U.S. v. United Foods, Inc., 533 U.S. 405 (2001), a tax on generic mushroom handlers that was used, in part, to subsidize generic advertising to promote mushroom sales was found to violate the First Amendment. Harris v. McRae, 448 U.S. 297 (1980) upheld the Hyde Amendment, which severely limited the use of federal funds to reimburse the cost of abortions under the medicaid program. Prince v. Massachusettes, 321 U.S. 158 (1944) upheld state child labor laws over a freedom of religion claim by a mother who brought her child "street preaching." Certain other licensing requirements and secular regulations impose burdens on religious practice. *See e.g.*, Braunfeld v. Brown, 366 U.S. 599 (1961); Gallagher v. Crown Kosher Super Market, 366 U.S. 617 (1961); McGowan v. Maryland, 366 U.S. 420 (1961); Two Guys from Harrison-Allentown, Inc. v. McGinley, 366 U.S. 582 (1961); Murdock v. Pennsylvania, 319 U.S. 105 (1943). First Amendment issues have been intermingled with right-to-work issues in *Schware v. Board of Bar* Examiners, 353 U.S. 232 (1957) and *Barsky v. Board of Regents*, 347 U.S. 442 (1954). Each of these examples illustrates an area of debate in which both economic and individual interests are at stake, and each case defies any attempt to neatly cabin these interests into one category or the other.

It is perhaps due to the amorphous nature of commercial behavior that the Commerce Clause has proven to be such a fertile basis for congressional legislation.[175]

E. **Meyer v. Nebraska,** *A Counter-Example*

The 1923 Supreme Court decision in *Meyer v. Nebraska*[176] is a useful example of constitutional adjudication prior to the adoption of the individual and economic rights dichotomy. Here, the Court considered a Nebraska law that prohibited teaching foreign languages in public schools prior to the eighth grade.[177] The Court struck down the statute as a violation of "liberty" as guaranteed by the Fourteenth Amendment.[178] Justice McReynolds, in a slight, four-page opinion, commented on this "liberty" with no apparent discrimination between rights of an economic and individual nature.

> Without doubt, it denotes not merely freedom from bodily restraint but also the right of the individual to contract, to engage in any of the common occupations of life, to acquire useful knowledge, to marry, establish a home and bring up children, to worship God according to dictates of his own conscience, and generally to enjoy those privileges long recognized by common law as essential to the orderly pursuit of happiness by free men.[179]

---

175 As most administrative enabling acts are passed under Congress' power to regulate commerce, this authority could be seen as the catalyst for the proliferation of the modern administrative state. Furthermore, it is difficult to conceive an overt human action that cannot be said to effect commerce. Even sexual intercourse, one of man's most intimate acts, often involves products purchased in the market place, such as prophylactics or contraceptives. More so, intercourse may have the most magnificent economic effects when such products are not used. Even abstaining from sex entirely could be said to effect commerce, as demand for sexual accoutrements would diminish and appetite for substitutes may rise. As Justice McReynolds has observed, "[a]lmost anything -- marriage, birth, death -- may in some fashion affect commerce." NLRB v. Jones & Laughlin Steel Corp., 301 U.S. 1, 99 (1937) (McReynolds, J., dissenting, joined by Van Devanter, Sutherland, and Butler, JJ.). In response to Justice Hughes' expansive view of the Commerce Clause, Justice McReynolds later argued that "So construed, the power to regulate interstate commerce brings within the ambit of federal control most if not all activities of the Nation . . . ." NLRB v. Fainblatt, 306 U.S. 601, 610 (1939) (McReynolds, J., dissenting, joined by Butler, J.).

176 262 U.S. 390 (1923).

177 *Id.* at 397. Under this law, Robert Meyer was convicted for teaching German to a ten year-old student. *Id.* at 396.

178 *Id.* at 403.

179 *Id.* at 399.

The Court evidently found teaching to be within the "orderly pursuit of happiness" and recognized the interests of both Mr. Meyer and the parents who employed him. "Plaintiff in error taught this language in school as part of his occupation. His right thus to teach and the right of parents to engage him so to instruct their children, we think, are within the liberty of the [Fourteenth A]mendment."[180]

The *Meyer* Court, perhaps rightly so, made no attempt to frame the question as either an individual or economic rights problem. Certainly, some may argue that the law at issue in *Meyer* is nothing more than a form of occupational licensing, an all too common incarnation of economic regulation. And perhaps Mr. Meyer *was* motivated by economic interests. On the other hand, maybe Mr. Meyer was motivated by an affinity for the German language, or even political incentives, such as promoting peaceful relations among foreign nations through common communication. In any event, the interests of the parents who employed Mr. Meyer cannot likely be considered exclusively commercial. More likely, these parents were interested in providing a well-rounded education for their children. Is the mere presence of financial compensation enough to taint the transaction as commercial?

Instead of conducting an inquisition into the motives of the actors, the *Meyer* Court recognized that legislation may have an impact on multiple spheres of human interest, such as the right to contract for employment, the right to contract for services, and even the "natural duty of the parent to give his children education."[181] In this instance, the Court made no attempt to apply the distinction between so-called individual and economic rights. Unfortunately, subsequent cases would not employ such a holistic view of constitutional rights.

III. ECONOMIC RIGHTS JURISPRUDENCE DIMINISHES PROTECTION FOR INDIVIDUAL RIGHTS

To uphold the sweeping new economic regulation of the Progressive Era, the Court constructed an unprecedented framework of legislative deference.[182] Perhaps due to the difficulty of distinguishing economic and noneconomic action,[183] the Court has been unable to confine its capitulations to issues of so-called economic rights. Rather, this philosophy of deference has spilled-over into rights more commonly considered individual in nature, such as access to medication and reproductive rights. The ultimate irony is that the system of deference advocated by early twentieth-century progressives in order to quash

[180] 262 U.S. at 400.

[181] *Id.*

economic rights is the very system through which many individual rights, championed by modern liberals, have met their demise.

Although sacking economic rights was the impetus for the rational basis test,[184] it is commonly applied to rights not enumerated in the text of the Constitution, including individual rights.[185] Thus, claims of unenumerated individual rights, such as access to physician assisted suicide, access to medical marijuana, and homosexual rights, are all subject to the rational basis test, the most flaccid standard of review.[186] Even reproductive rights, perhaps the holiest of liberal institutions, has suffered diminished protection as a result of the Court's earlier contempt for economic rights.[187]

A. Physician-Assisted Suicide

In *Washington v. Glucksberg*, the Court considered the constitutionality of a Washington statute that criminalized aiding in the suicide of another.[188] Although this issue is more properly considered individual in nature, it would ultimately be felled by the rational basis test, which was established to dispense with claims of economic rights.

In *Glucksberg*, the Court first rejected the argument that physician-assisted suicide was a fundamental right protected by the Due Process Clause.[189] Once

---

182 *See supra* Part II.

183 *See supra* Part III.

184 *See, e.g.*, Donald C. Guy & James E. Holloway, *The Direction of Regulatory Takings Analysis in the Post-Lochner Era*, 102 DICK. L. REV. 327, 333 (1998) ("Carolene Products distinguished economic and property rights from fundamental rights.").

185 *See infra* Part III.A-D; *see, e.g.,* Gonzales v. Raich, 545 U.S. 1 (2005) (applying the rational basis test to an asserted right to medical marijuana); Lawrence v. Texas, 539 U.S. 558 (2003) (applying the rational basis test to the unenumerated right to homosexual sodomy); Washington v. Glucksberg, 521 U.S. 702 (1997) (applying the rational basis test to the unenumerated right to physician assisted suicide); Michael H. v. Gerald D., 491 U.S. 110, 131 (1989) (applying the "rational relationship" test to a child's unenumerated right to rebut the presumption of her legitimacy).

186 *See* Neily, *supra* note 47.

187 *See infra* Part III.C-D.

188 521 U.S. 702, 705 (1997) (considering WASH. REV. CODE § 9A.36.060(1) (1994) ("A person is guilty of promoting a suicide attempt when he knowingly causes or aids another person to attempt suicide.")). Here, four physicians, three patients, and a nonprofit organization challenged the Washington statute, claiming that it was facially unconstitutional as a deprivation of their due process rights. *Id.* at 707-08.

189 *Id.* at 728. In making a determination, the Court, speaking through Chief Justice Rehnquist, first conducted a lengthy review of our history of prohibiting assisted suicide. *Id.* at 710-19. Next, the Court noted that the due process clause only protects as fundamental a right "deeply rooted in this Nation's history and tradition[.]" *Id.* at 720-21 (quoting Moore v. City of East

the right in question was deemed nonfundamental, the Court deployed the rational basis standard of review. To survive, the statute only needed to be rationally related to a legitimate government interest, a standard the Court found was "unquestionably met here."[190] To support this finding, the Court pointed to state interests such as the preservation of human life[191] and protecting the integrity and ethics of the medical profession.[192] The plaintiffs acknowledged these interests, but claimed they could be better served by the regulation, rather than the prohibition, of assisted suicide.[193] However, as the right in question was only being examined under the rational basis test, the Court explained that the inquiry was "limited to the question whether the State's prohibition is rationally related to legitimate state interests."[194] Thus, under the framework of due process analysis suggested by *Carolene Products*, a vestige of the Court's scorn for economic rights, access to physician-assisted suicide, a right more properly considered individual in nature, found no meaningful protection. Instead, the advocates of this right were visited with the same brand of dismissive justice that earlier proponents of economic rights had received: "The legislature knows best."

That this issue can be couched in terms of partisan ideology is no surprise. A right to assisted suicide is chiefly concerned with the person, so, generally, one would expect liberals to advocate its protection and conservatives to crusade for its regulation. In this expectation, one would not be disappointed. To illustrate, groups that filed amici briefs in *Glucksberg* in favor of the plaintiffs included the ACLU, the Center for Reproductive Law & Policy, Gay Men's Health Crisis, and the National Women's Health Network.[195] In contrast, amici were filed on behalf of the government by the American Center for Law and Justice, the Christian Legal Society, the National Right to Life Committee, and U.S. Senator Orrin Hatch.[196] The ultimate irony is that an issue close to the hearts of many modern liberals fell victim to the framework of legislative deference championed by their ancestors in power during the Progressive Era. Notably, the *Glucksberg* decision was unanimous, suggesting that even the

---

Cleveland, 431 U.S. 494, 503 (1977)). Ultimately, the Court concluded that "the asserted 'right' to assistance in committing suicide is not a fundamental liberty interest protected by the Due Process Clause." 521 U.S. at 728. The Court drew the same conclusion with respect to the Equal Protection Clause in *Vacco v. Quill.* 521 U.S. 793 (1997).

190 521 U.S. at 728.

191 *Id.* at 728-29.

192 *Id.* at 731.

193 *Id.* at 728, n.21.

194 *Id.*

195 *Id.*

196 *Id.*

liberal-leaning jurists on the bench – Justices Stevens, Breyer, Ginsburg, and Souter – could not find meaningful protection under modern due process jurisprudence.[197]

Had the earlier analysis of the *Meyer* Court prevailed, the *Glucksberg* plaintiffs might have relied on a host of interests involved, such as the right of the patients to contract for services and the right of physicians to seek gainful employment, as well as the right of an individual to end his own life. But the jurisprudence used to subjugate economic rights effectively removed these arguments from the Court's consideration, leaving it to question only whether the legislation was rational. At a minimum, a more searching standard of review, exhibited by the *Meyer* Court, would examine whether the legislation being scrutinized actually served the State's purported interests. Of course, it is uncertain whether the asserted right to physician-assisted suicide would be protected under a different framework. Under the rational basis test, however, its demise was almost certain.

B. *Medicinal Cannabis*

The U.S. Supreme Court decision in *Gonzales v. Raich*[198] is a striking example of economic jurisprudence beaching itself on the sandy shores of an asserted individual right, namely, access to physician-prescribed medicinal cannabis. After being subject to a raid by Federal Marshals, plaintiffs Raich and Monson[199] challenged the Controlled Substances Act[200] ("CSA") as applied to

---

197 The OYEZ Project, Washington v. Glucksberg, 521 U.S. 702 (1997), *available at* http://www.oyez.org/cases/case?case=1990-1999/1996/1996_96_110.

198 545 U.S. 1 (2005). *Raich*, of course, upheld the Controlled Substances Act as a valid congressional prohibition of "the intrastate, noncommercial cultivation and possession of cannabis for personal medical purposes as recommended by a patient's physician pursuant to valid California state law." *Id.* at 8 (2005) (quoting Raich v. Ashcroft, 352 F.3d 1222, 1228 (9th Cir. 2003)).

199 Angel Raich and Diane Monson used medical marijuana to ameliorate symptoms related to a host of illnesses. Specifically, Raich suffers from "an inoperable brain tumor, life-threatening weight loss, a seizure disorder, nausea, and several chronic pain disorders. Appellant Monson suffers from severe chronic back pain and constant, painful muscle spasms caused by a degenerative disease of the spine." Raich v. Ashcroft, 352 F.3d 1222, 1225 (9th Cir. 2003). On August 15, 2002, Drug Enforcement Agents came to Monson's home and seized and destroyed her cannabis plants. *Id.* Subsequently, Raich and Monson sought injunctive and declaratory relief prohibiting the enforcement of the CSA on the grounds that their behavior did not constitute commerce within the scope of the Commerce Clause. *Id.*

200 21 U.S.C. § 801. The CSA sought to combat the traffic of illicit drugs by establishing a closed regulatory system, which made unlawful the manufacture, distribution, or possession of controlled substance, such as marijuana, in a manner not prescribed by the CSA. In passing the CSA, Congress was particularly concerned with preventing "the diversion of drugs from

medical cannabis used in accordance with California's Compassionate Use Act.[201] Although acknowledging that the Plaintiffs' actions were both *intrastate* and *noncommercial*,[202] the Court, nonetheless, found that the CSA was a valid use of Congress' power to regulate *interstate commerce*.[203] To the uninitiated, the application of the CSA to activity that is admittedly neither interstate nor commercial would appear patently offensive. This apparent anomaly, however, is easily explained by economic rights jurisprudence.

In upholding the CSA, Justice Stevens relied heavily on the Court's 1942 decision in *Wickard v. Filburn*.[204] Wickard challenged the Agricultural Adjustment Act of 1938 (the "Act"), which was classic New Deal legislation, limiting the volume of wheat any individual farm was permitted to grow.[205] In deciding that Congress could even regulate wheat grown for personal consumption, Justice Jackson declared that "even if appellee's activity be local and though it may not be regarded as commerce, it may still, whatever its nature, be reached by Congress if it exerts a substantial economic effect on interstate commerce."[206] The *Raich* Court directly quoted this language from *Wickard* and found that privately cultivated cannabis could have such a

---

legitimate to illicit channels." 545 U.S. at 12-14 (citing United States v. Moore, 423 U.S. 122, 135 (1975); H. R. Rep., at 22.).

201 CAL. HEALTH & SAFETY CODE ANN. § 11362.5. The act provided immunity for physicians. "Notwithstanding any other provision of law, no physician in this state shall be punished, or denied any right or privilege, for having recommended marijuana to a patient for medical purposes." *Id.* § 11362.5(c). Patients and caregivers were also protected under the act.

> Section 11357, relating to the possession of marijuana, and Section 11358, relating to the cultivation of marijuana, shall not apply to a patient, or to a patient's primary caregiver, who possesses or cultivates marijuana for the personal medical purposes of the patient upon the written or oral recommendation or approval of a physician.

Id. § 11362.5(d).

202 *Id.* at 8. Raich received locally grown cannabis from caregivers free of charge, and Monson personally cultivated her own cannabis. *Id.* at 7.

203 *Id.* at 9.

204 317 U.S. 111 (1942). *Wickard* upheld the Agricultural Adjustment Act of 1938 (the "Act"), which,. *Id.* at 115. , but he sowed 23 acres and harvested 239 bushels, which constituted farm marketing excess, subject to a penalty of 49 cents a bushel, or $ 117.11 total. *Id.* at 114-15.

205 The regulations were passed in an effort to stymie excess supply of crops. *Id.* at 114-15. They established a wheat acreage allotment of 11.1 acres and a normal yield of 20.1 bushels of wheat per acre for Filburn's 1941 wheat crop. *Id.* Filburn was charged with violating the Act and challenged this violation, urging that his wheat crop was grown wholly for consumption on the farm and, thus, not subject to regulations on commerce. *Id.* at 118.

206 545 U.S. at 17 (quoting Wickard v. Filburn, 317 U.S. 111, 125 (1942)).

"substantial economic effect on interstate commerce" because of the ease with which homegrown cannabis could slip into the illicit drug market.[207]

Although the *Wickard* Court contemplated federal regulation aimed at arguably economic behavior, wheat production,[208] the *Raich* Court was forced to apply the same deferential standard to a virtually indistinguishable case involving a right more at home among individual liberties, access to physician-prescribed medication.[209] Indeed, the plaintiffs in each case were engaged in nearly identical behavior, growing a crop at home for personal consumption. Thus, if Congress could regulate Wickard's wheat, so too could Congress regulate Raich and Monson's weed. Perhaps the cases can be distinguished because Wickard was also selling wheat on the open market. Regardless, this distinction was too slight to warrant even a nod from the Court. At a minimum, these two cases show a connection between economic and noneconomic action; greater respect by the earlier Court for the economic rights of farmers may have resulted in more significant protection for the individual rights of terminally ill patients. Instead, by zealously upholding economic regulation, the Court weakened protections for both individual and economic rights.

Politically, the case resulted in a somewhat topsy-turvy decision. The liberals of the Court, Justices Stevens, Ginsburg, Souter, and Breyer, joined by Justice Scalia, voted *against* access to medicinal cannabis. Meanwhile, the conservatives of the Court, Justices Thomas, Rehnquist, and O'Connor, voted *for* access to medicinal cannabis. When analyzing the problem through the lens of economic rights, however, the apparent anomaly is easily explained. The liberal justices were unwilling, and the conservative justices all too willing, to curtail Congress' power to regulate commerce. If Congress was unable to regulate the actions of Raich and Monson, the modern framework of sweeping economic regulations might be next on the chopping block. In this instance, it should not go unnoticed that the exact piece of *economic* regulation enacted by Progressives of the New Deal era proved fatal to medicinal cannabis, an *individual* right championed by modern liberals.

C. Access to Contraception

The enigmatic distinction between individual and economic rights has also left its mark on reproductive rights. The Court in *Griswold v. Connecticut*[210] upheld the right of an individual to purchase and use contraceptives.[211] It did so, however,

207 *Id.* at 30-33.
208 317 U.S. at 125.
209 545 U.S. at 8.
210 381 U.S. 479 (1965).
211 *Id.* at 480.

on an unstable and intellectually dishonest foundation in order to distinguish the case from the unbroken line of economic rights decisions, leading the Honorable Louis H. Pollak to diplomatically refer to the opinion as a "non-starter."[212] From the outset of the opinion, Justice Douglas vowed not to rest the decision upon substantive due process rights,[213] which had been the basis

---

212 Hon. Louis H. Pollak, *"Liberty": Enumerated Rights? Unenumerated Rights? Penumbral Rights? Other?,"* 8 U. PA. J. CONST. L. 905, 908 (2006). *See also*, Robert H. Bork, *Neutral Principles and Some First Amendment Problems*, 47 IND. L. J. 1, at 9 (1971) ("Griswold, then, is an unprincipled decision, both in the way in which it derives a new constitutional right and in the way it defines that right, or rather fails to define it.").

213 381 U.S. at 481. In examining the propriety of this decision, it is profitable to explore Justice Douglas' exact language declaring that the case would not rest upon due process rights.

Coming to the merits, we are met with a wide range of questions that implicate the Due Process Clause of the Fourteenth Amendment. Overtones of some arguments suggest that *Lochner v. State of New York* should be our guide. But we decline that invitation as we did in [many cases]. We do not sit as a super-legislature to determine the wisdom, need, and propriety of laws that touch economic problems, business affairs, or social conditions. This law, however, operates directly on an intimate relation of husband and wife and their physician's role in one aspect of that relation.

Id. at 481. In truth, the invitation to which Justice Douglas refers was never issued. Pollak, *supra* note 212, at 910. Counsel for appellants, Thomas I. Emerson, stated during oral argument that "we are not asking this Court to revive Lochner against New York." *Id.*; Transcript of Oral Argument, Griswold v. Connecticut (Mar. 29, 1965), *reprinted in* 61 LANDMARK BRIEFS AND ARGUMENTS OF THE SUPREME COURT OF THE UNITED STATES 413 (Philip B. Kurland & Gerhard Casper eds., 1975). Then the following colloquy took place:

> The Court: It sounds to me like you're asking us to follow the constitutional philosophy of that case.
> Mr. Emerson: No, Your Honor. We are asking you to follow the philosophy of Meyer against Nebraska and Pierce against the Society of Sisters, which dealt with - Meyer against Nebraska
> The Court: Was the one that held it was unconstitutional, as I recall it, for a state to try to regulate the size of loaves of bread -
> Mr. Emerson: No, no, no.
> The Court: - because people were being defrauded; was that it?
> Mr. Emerson: That was the Lochner case, Your Honor. Meyer against Nebraska held that it was unconstitutional for a state to enact a law prohibiting the teaching of the German language to children who had not passed the eighth grade. And Pierce against the Society of Sisters held that it was unconstitutional for a state to prevent the operation of private schools in a state. And those were both due process cases, were decided as due process cases. . . . All were due process cases which related to individual rights and liberties, and we distinguish those from the cases which involved commercial operations like Lochner against New York and West Coast Hotel against Parrish. We make that very definite distinction.

for the Court's previous protection of economic liberties.[214] By closing off this avenue of analysis, Justice Douglas was forced to find the favored right in unusual places, an approach that has proved to be a precarious basis protection.

Specifically, the *Griswold* Court declared unconstitutional a Connecticut statute that prohibited the use and distribution of contraceptives. In order to avoid breaking his pledge to avoid the Due Process Clause, Justice Douglas asserted that certain rights are protected within penumbra formed by emanations from specific guarantees in the Bill of Rights.[215] The right to privacy, argued Justice Douglas, was one such right.[216] As Justice Douglas further explained, prohibiting married couples from using contraceptives violated this penumbral right to privacy. "Would we allow the police to search the sacred precincts of marital bedrooms for telltale signs of the use of contraceptives? The very idea is repulsive to the notions of privacy surrounding the marriage relationship."[217]

Thus, to avoid relying on the unfashionable Due Process Clause, Justice Douglas was forced first to apply a disingenuous label (privacy) and second to find protection for the proffered right in a fantastic and elaborate hodgepodge

---

Id. Thus, Mr. Emerson appealed to the dichotomy between individual and economic rights in an effort to distinguish his case from the disfavored economic rights due process cases.

214 *See, e.g.*, Lochner v. New York, 198 U.S. 45 (1905).

215 *Id.* at 484.

216 *Id.* at 484-85 (citations omitted).

> The right of association contained in the penumbra of the First Amendment is one, as we have seen. The Third Amendment in its prohibition against the quartering of soldiers 'in any house' in time of peace without the consent of the owner is another facet of that privacy. The Fourth Amendment explicitly affirms the 'right of the people to be secure in their persons, houses, papers, and effects, against unreasonable searches and seizures.' The Fifth Amendment in its Self-Incrimination Clause enables the citizen to create a zone of privacy which government may not force him to surrender to his detriment. The Ninth Amendment provides: 'The enumeration in the Constitution, of certain rights, shall not be construed to deny or disparage others retained by the people.' The Fourth and Fifth Amendments were described . . . as protection against all governmental invasions 'of the sanctity of a man's home and the privacies of life.' We recently referred . . . to the Fourth Amendment as creating a 'right to privacy, no less important than any other right carefully and particularly reserved to the people.'

Id. Justice Douglas cites *Pierce v. Society of Sisters* and *Meyer v. Nebraska* as upholding the right of association and privacy under the First and Fourteenth Amendments, but neither decision so much as mentioned the First Amendment. Pollak, *supra* note 212, at 914. Nor could they have because they both predated the incorporation of the First Amendment against the states in 1925. *Id.*

217 *Id.* at 485-86.

of other rights. What was really at issue, of course, was not privacy. It was liberty of action. But Justice Douglas, who lived through the *Lochner*-era, realized that liberty of action, if recognized in this context, would be impossible to distinguish from liberty of action in the economic context. As such, the Court would be forced to recognize less popular rights, such as the right to contract freely, to start a business, or to work as much as one pleases.

Surely the right to use contraceptives at issue in *Griswold* would have been safer under the broad protections of the Due Process Clause. As Justice Harlan's concurrence recognizes, "the proper constitutional inquiry… is whether this Connecticut statute infringes the Due Process Clause of the Fourteenth Amendment because the enactment violates basic values 'implicit in the concept of ordered liberty.'"[218] Instead, by relying on privacy, *Griswold* would seem to condone a prohibition on the sale, rather than use, of contraceptives; such a ban would be enforced in places of business and would not require police to "search the sacred precincts of marital bedrooms." Subsequent cases have continued to find protection for access to contraceptives.[219] However, the future of such rights based on an unstable foundation is uncertain.[220] Furthermore, these rights could only be strengthened by proper respect for a full spectrum of due process rights, including economic liberties. Indeed, the right to *use* contraceptives is of little use without the right to *purchase* contraceptives. The approach employed by the *Meyer* Court would consider a host of interests, including economic rights, such as the right of the clinic operator to choose a lawful calling, the right of the pharmacist to tender his wares, or the right of the consumer to purchase useful products. Under this holistic view, the right of access to contraceptives would be covered in a protective shroud of constitutional rights, all interlocking to provide meaningful protection to each other.

D. Partial Birth Abortion

---

218 381 U.S. at 500 (Harlan, J., concurring) (quoting Palko v. Connecticut, 302 U.S. 319, 325 (1937)).

219 *See, e.g.*, Eisenstadt v. Baird, 405 U.S. 438 (1972); Roe v. Wade, 410 U.S. 113 (1973); Carey v. Population Services Intl., 431 U.S. 678 (1977).

220 *See infra* Part I.D.

Even more recently, the Court's treatment of economic rights has implicated one of the individual rights most revered among the political left, access to abortion. In 2003, under its power to regulate interstate commerce, Congress passed into law the Partial-Birth Abortion Ban Act[221] (the "PBABA"), which prohibits an abortive procedure medically known as intact dilation and extraction. The plaintiffs in *Gonzales v. Carhart*[222] challenged the PBABA under the modern framework of abortion rights. Finding that it did not present an undue burden to a woman's right to an abortion, the Court upheld the PBABA as a valid congressional act.

The modern right to access to abortion can be traced back to the right to privacy found in *Griswold v. Connecticut.*[223] Justice Douglas, of course, constructed the right to privacy in *Griswold* in order to avoid relying on the Due Process Clause, which had been the Court's previous basis for invalidating so much economic regulation. However, under the framework of a right to privacy, erected to expedite the evisceration of economic rights, the right to partial birth abortion found no meaningful protection. Of course, one can only speculate as to whether the PBABA would have survived under the more robust Due Process Clause in existence prior to the bifurcation of rights; nonetheless, the Court's distaste for economic rights foreclosed several arguments for the *Carhart* plaintiffs.

221 18 U.S.C. § 1531 (2003). The PBA Ban provides that

> [a]ny physician who, in or affecting interstate or foreign commerce, knowingly performs a partial-birth abortion and thereby kills a human fetus shall be fined under this title or imprisoned not more than 2 years, or both. This subsection does not apply to a partial-birth abortion that is necessary to save the life of a mother whose life is endangered by a physical disorder, physical illness, or physical injury, including a life-endangering physical condition caused by or arising from the pregnancy itself. This subsection takes effect 1 day after the enactment [enacted Nov. 5, 2003].

18 U.S.C. § 1531(a) (2003).

222 550 U.S. 124 (2007).

223 *Eisenstadt v. Baird* extended to unmarried individuals the right to privacy recognized by *Griswold v. Connecticut.* Eisenstadt v. Baird, 405 U.S. 438 (1972). *Roe v. Wade* then declared that "[i]f the right of privacy means anything, it is the right of the individual, married or single, to be free from unwarranted governmental intrusion into matters so fundamentally affecting a person as the decision whether to bear or beget a child." Roe v. Wade, 410 U.S. 113, 153 (1973). *Planned Parenthood v. Casey* then affirmed *Roe's* holding but altered it to prohibit states from imposing an "undue burden" on access to abortion. Planned Parenthood v. Casey, 505 U.S. 833 (1992). Finally, in *Stenberg v. Carhart,* the Court struck down a state-imposed ban on partial birth abortion, according to the Court, imposed an undue burden on access to other types of abortions and lacked an exception for the health of the mother. Stenberg v. Carhart, 530 U.S. 914, 930-51 (2000).

A theory of rights that equally respects economic and individual interests, as exhibited by the *Meyer* Court, would consider a host of interests encompassed by the concept of "liberty" and not an artificial analysis of whether a right is "fundamental." As the *Meyer* Court would have recognized, the rights at stake in *Gonzales v. Carhart* are diverse. One may frame the debate in terms of a physician's right to pursue lawful employment, a consumer's right to purchase services, or the right of individuals to freely contract among themselves. The subjugation of economic rights, however, has essentially removed these arguments from the Court's consideration and left individuals to grasp instead at a guest list of favored rights, such as privacy.

Access to partial birth abortion could also find more significant protection if economic rights were more respected within the realm of Commerce Clause jurisprudence. Indeed, even though the parties did not raise the issue, Justice Thomas' concurrence in *Gonzales v. Carhart*, joined by Justice Scalia, signaled an openness to the argument that the PBABA exceeded Congress' power to regulate interstate commerce.[224]

Originally, "commerce" consisted solely of "selling, buying, and bartering, as well as transporting for these purposes."[225] Thus, under its power to regulate commerce, Congress could only regulate "selling, buying, and bartering" and not activities such as manufacturing and agriculture.[226] Perhaps due to the amorphous nature of economic actions, or perhaps due to the Court's eagerness to uphold economic regulation, the Commerce Clause now applies to industry in nearly all its forms.[227] Justice Stevens even questioned during oral arguments whether the PBABA, passed under Congress' power to regulate commerce, would apply to free clinics.[228] Justice Stevens, author of the Court's

---

224 550 U.S. at 169 (Thomas, J., concurring) ("I also note that whether the Act constitutes a permissible exercise of Congress' power under the Commerce Clause is not before the Court. The parties did not raise or brief that issue; it is outside the question presented; and the lower courts did not address it.") (citations omitted).

225 *See supra* note 142 and accompanying text.

226 *See supra* note 143 and 143 and accompanying text.

227 From 1945 to 1995, the Supreme Court did not strike down a single piece of legislation on the grounds that Congress surpassed its Commerce Clause powers. Grant S. Nelson & Robert J. Pushaw, Jr., *Rethinking the Commerce Clause: Applying First Principles to Uphold Federal Commercial Regulations but Preserve State Control Over Social Issues*, 85 IOWA L. REV. 1, 83-84 (1999);

228 Transcript of Oral Argument at 21-22, Gonzales v. Planned Parenthood (Nov. 8, 2006) (No. 05-1382).

> JUSTICE STEVENS: General Clement, [t]hat brings up a question I was intending to ask you. I notice the finding says nothing about interstate commerce but the statute says any physician who in or affecting interstate commerce performs the procedures. Does that mean that the procedure is

majority opinion in *Raich*, could have easily answered his own question. *Raich*, relying on *Wickard*, upheld the application of the Commerce Clause to noncommercial intrastate action. Thus, the PBABA would seem to apply even to clinics that do not operate for profit.

And with an expansive view of the Commerce Clause, the application of the PBABA to free clinics is only natural; any behavior can be said to effect commerce on some level. To uphold a ban on partial birth abortions, even in free clinics, a court need only hypothesize about the various ways in which partial birth abortions may affect interstate commerce. Undoubtedly, this procedure requires the use of products – from catheters to curettes, forceps to fetoscopes – that are shipped in interstate commerce. And by the same rationale used in *Wickard* and *Raich*, abortions at free clinics may affect the national commercial market for abortions by reducing their demand in the open market. Most significantly, an abortion may be said to effect commerce by preventing the consumption of goods accompanying the birth, and life, of a potential consumer. With any of these speculations and an expansive view of the Commerce Clause, the constitutionality of the PBABA as a valid exercise of Congress' power to regulate interstate commerce is practically a foregone conclusion.

However, under a more modest interpretation of the Commerce Clause, consistent with meaningful protection for economic rights, Congress would not have the power to prohibit partial birth abortions. In fact, the Court in *United States v. Lopez*[229] and *United States v. Morrison*[230] made broad strides toward the curtailment of the Commerce Clause. Certainly, if the Commerce Clause did not reach manufacturing or agriculture, as was the case before the subjugation

---

> performed in a free clinic, as opposed to a profit organization, it would not be covered?
>
> GENERAL CLEMENT: Justice Stevens, I don't think we have taken, the Federal Government hasn't taken a definitive position on that. I think it could be interpreted either way. I think my understanding is the face context, a free clinic would be covered. There's not a jurisdictional element in the face statute. So there may be differences as, in application.
>
> JUSTICE STEVENS: But how could the Commerce Clause justify application to a free clinic? I don't understand.

Id.

229 514 U.S. 549 (1995) (striking down congressional regulation of gun possession near schools as beyond Congress' power to regulate commerce).

230 529 U.S. 598 (2000) (striking down congressional regulation of domestic violence as beyond Congress' power to regulate commerce).

of economic rights, the PBABA would also be beyond Congress' power to regulate commerce and, thus, be found unconstitutional.

Gonzales v. Carhart provides an important illustration of the interconnection of individual and economic rights. Here, the legislative deference preached throughout the Progressive Era to justify sweeping economic regulation led to the marginalization of the Due Process Clause and the expansion of the Commerce Clause. As a result, plaintiffs, such as those in *Carhart*, are left with a smaller shield, and Congress a larger sword, when congressional action and individual rights inevitably clash. If nothing else, *Carhart* shows that the subjugation of economic rights has led to diminished protection for certain individual rights. By the same reasoning, more meaningful protection for economic rights may lead to more significant protections for many individual rights. Not surprisingly, it is the conservative justices who are most likely to advocate stronger protection for economic rights.[231] Although it remains to be seen, it is noteworthy that on this one issue abortion rights activists may become bedfellows with conservative justices.

IV. DISCUSSION

A. Perhaps Economic Rights Are No Different From Individual Rights

Arguably, the distinction between individual and economic rights is a false one.[232] Rights spring forth from human interests, and human interests cannot

---

231 For example, in the majority opinions of *United States v. Lopez* and *United States v. Morrison* were Justices Thomas, Scalia, Rehnquist, Kennedy, and O'Connor. Dissenting in both were Justices Stevens, Ginsburg, Souter, and Breyer.

232 LAURENCE H. TRIBE, AMERICAN CONSTITUTIONAL LAW 1373-74 (2d. ed. 1988); Jonathan R. Macey, *Some Courses and Consequences of the Bifurcated Treatment of Economic Rights and 'Other' Rights Under the United States Constitution*, 9 SOC. PHIL. & POL. 141, 145-55 (1992); Joseph Becker, Note, *Procrustean Jurisprudence: An Austrian School Economic Critique of the Separation and Regulation of Liberties in the Twentieth Century*, 15 N. ILL. U. L. REV. 671, 705-712 (1995). Austrian Economics explains that the separation of liberties is a scientific impossibility because (1) all human action is economic; (2) all actions or liberty require property; (3) the regulation of property necessarily devalues the individual owner of property; (4) it is impossible to know the true motive of an actor and whether the action is an end or a mean; (5) judicial devaluation of economic liberties is inherently pareto inferior; and (6) resources required to engage in individual rights will be scarce if not protected by property rights and allocated by market mechanisms). *Id.* Becker also argues that the rights separation scheme creates uncertainty and economic stagnation as courts embracing this fallacy will produce arbitrary judicial decisions, causing spending to shift from investment to consumption and resulting in lower levels of economic growth. *Id.* at 712. From an Austrian Economics perspective, socio-economic regulation would not even pass the rational basis test because no legislature could rationally know that redistributionist legislation would result in a paraeto-superior exchange, unless,

be neatly splintered into purely economic or noneconomic categories.[233] Realistically, people are not comprised of diametrically opposed economic and noneconomic beings; thus, many human actions are motivated by a combination of economic and noneconomic interests.[234] As Professor Shiffrin would put it, "[a] person listening to commercial advertising is not hermetically sealed off from his or her place in the world -- as homo economicus."[235] As Justice Blackmun observed, the interests of contestants in a labor dispute may implicate the right to assemble as well as so-called economic rights.[236] Likewise, the motives of a political candidate or an independent retailer may consist of a mixture of economic and noneconomic interests. If the motive of the actor is even the right query, any attempt to capture the precise bounds of an actor's interests is surely rife with complications.[237]

More so, in a market economy, economic gains are no more than a mere commodification of one's ability to exercise individual liberties.[238] A taxi cab driver does not seek his paycheck as an end unto itself.[239] More likely, he is seeking the food it will allow him to purchase and the shelter he is able to provide for his family. Thus, any regulation on his so-called economic rights necessitates some measure of infringement on other activities considered to be noneconomic.[240]

Likewise, the ability to exercise many individual rights directly depends on having the economic wherewithal to purchase the necessary accoutrements. As

---

Becker muses, "minimizing societal wealth is the judicially desired 'rational' end." *Id.* at 714-16. *Cf.* PURDUE, REEXAMINATION OF DISTINCTION 1252 (noting the difficulty in distinguishing between conduct regulating rules versus loss allocation rules). "[C]ompensation and deterrence cannot be separated." *Id.*

This Article will focus on the argument that economic rights cannot be neatly distinguished from noneconomic rights as a matter of form. For a useful treatment of the related argument that economic rights are equally as important as noneconomic rights, *see, e.g.*, Siegan, *Protecting Economic Liberties*, *supra* note 9, at 473-81.

233 *See* LUDWIG VON MISES, HUMAN ACTION 13-14 (3d rev. ed. 1966).

234 *See* Shiffrin, *supra* note 84, at 1222.

235 *Id.* (criticizing the Court's decision in *Central Hudson* by arguing that "[t]hose who paid attention to Central Hudson's promotion of electricity did not process its message by shunting the message into an exclusive economic compartment entirely removed from all thinking about energy problems"). Likewise, Professor Shiffrin notes that it is "curious" to describe a divorce attorney's advertisement as relating solely to the listener's economic interests. *Id.*

236 425 U.S. at 763.

237 VON MISES, *supra* note 233, at 92-93, 96, 233-34.

238 *See* HANS-HERMANN HOPPE, A THEORY OF SOCIALISM AND CAPITALISM 15 (1989); Macey *supra* note 232, at 148.

239 *See* VON MISES, *supra* note 233, at 233-34.

240 *See* Hans-Hermann Hoppe, *The Ultimate Justification of the Private Property Ethic*, LIBERTY, Sept. 1988, at 21.

Murray Rothbard points out, "the human right of a free press is the property right to buy materials and then print leaflets or books and to sell them to those who are willing to buy."[241] Similarly, the right to use contraceptives depends upon the manufacturer having the right to produce contraceptives as well as the consumer having the right to purchase contraceptives.[242] We may enjoy as much privacy in the bedroom as we like, but the enjoyment of this right is necessarily diminished for some if the government remains free to ban the sale of erotic devices to adults, as Alabama has recently done.[243]

In *Lynch v. Household Finance Corp.*, Justice Stewart realized the fallacy of attempting to distinguish economic from personal rights.

> [T]he dichotomy between personal liberties and property rights is a false one. Property does not have rights. People have rights. The right to enjoy property without unlawful deprivation, no less than the right to speak or the right to travel, is in truth, a "personal" right, whether the "property" in question be a welfare check, a home, or a savings account. In fact, a fundamental interdependence exists between the personal right to liberty and the personal right in property. Neither could have meaning without the other. That rights in property are basic civil rights has long been recognized.[244]

In the parlance of our times, does a blogger engage in commercial speech when she posts a review of an album on her website? Perhaps so, according to the Federal Trade Commission; new regulations require bloggers to disclose endorsements and promotional items they have received.[245]

At their core, economic rights and individual rights share the same concern – liberty of action. The naked truth is that some actions for economic gains are indistinguishable from actions motivated by other concerns.[246] Just as no court

---

241 MURRAY N. ROTHBARD, FOR A NEW LIBERTY 43 (rev. ed. 1978).

242 *See* Hoppe, *supra.*

243 Williams v. Atty General of Ala, 378 F.3d 1232 (11th Cir. 2004), *aff'd*, 478 F.3d 1316 (11th Cir. 2007) (upholding a ban on the commercial distribution of certain sexual devices and finding the law rationally related to the government interest of preserving and promoting public morality).

244 Lynch v. Household Finance Corp., 405 U.S. 538, 552 (1972).

245 FTC Guidelines Concerning the Use of Endorsements and Testimonials in Advertising, 16 C.F.R. § 255 (2009), *available at* http://ftc.gov/os/2009/10/091005endorsementguidesfnnotice.pdf.

246 VON MISES, *supra* note 233, at 92-93, 96, 233-34; *see supra* Part II.

can define commercial speech as separate from political speech,[247] no legislature can purport to distinguish labor for money from a labor of love. As far back as 1688, John Locke understood that there was no clear distinction between property and liberty interests, instead referring to "lives, liberties, and estates, which I call by the general Name, 'Property.'"[248] As long as laws are aimed at actions and not motives, any attempt to adjudicate rights based on economic or noneconomic categories will be a mere semantic flimflam.[249]

As a testament to the inextricable link between the two, the jurisprudence attempting to distinguish and dismiss economic rights has had a visible impact on many rights more commonly considered individual in nature.[250] The Court's zealous evisceration of economic rights, such as freely contracting or earning an honest living, has diminished protections for even the most sacred of individual rights.[251] Although conceived to dispense claims of economic rights, the rational basis test has proven to be the demise of rights more properly traditionally individual, such as access to physician-assisted suicide and medicinal cannabis.[252] Likewise, the hearty expansion of the Commerce Clause has been the basis for congressional regulation of decidedly noneconomic action.[253] This outcome, however, does not surprise one who understands the interconnected nature of so-called individual and economic rights;[254] a government that has been granted carte blanche to regulate one sphere can play fast and loose with

---

247 *See supra* Part I.B.

248 John Locke, The Second Treatise of Government § 123 (Peter Laslett ed., 2d ed., Cambridge Univ. Press 1967) (1688).

249 M. C. Jensen and W. H. Meckling, "Theory of the Firm: Managerial Behavior, Agency Costs and Ownership Structure," *Journal of Financial Economics*, vol. 3 (1976), at 307, n. 6 ("the introduction of the wholly false distinction between property rights and human rights in many policy discussions is surely one of the all time great semantic flimflams").

250 Walter Dellinger, *The Indivisibility of Economic Rights and Personal Liberty*, 2004 CATO SUP. CT. REV. 9, 13 (2004) (arguing that the Constitution protects both economic and individual liberties and that the Court's repudiation of economic rights has weakened the foundation of personal rights by forcing "inept" opinions, such as *Griswold v. Connecticut*). Dellinger notes that "[t]he failure to protect either economic or personal liberty inevitably weakens both" because deference to the legislature on economic matters has taken away the argument that the government must justify laws amounting to an intrusion upon unenumerated liberties. *Id.* at 18. *See also* Macey *supra* note 232, at 157 (arguing that the Court's failure to protect economic liberties has led to the proliferation of special interest legislation).

251 *See supra* Part III.C-D.

252 *See supra* Part III.A-B.

253 *See supra* Part II.D.

254 *See supra* Part IV; Macey *supra* note 232, at 149 ("The political reality is that noneconomic freedom does not last long where economic freedom has been destroyed.); Margaret Jan Radin, *Property and Personhood*, 34 STAN. L. REV. 957, 1014-15 (1982) (arguing that economic rights facilitate the exercise of speech and voting).

nearly all human rights.[255] Thus, an attempt to safeguard one group of interests, while offering the other a subordinate place in the hierarchy of rights, may have the collateral effect of sacrificing both to some extent.[256] Perhaps the selective protection of rights creates a sort of Maginot Line, easily circumvented by excessive regulation in less favored areas.[257] Even while professing bold protection for speech, a society may nonetheless approve of a host of economic regulations -- such as zoning ordinances, licensing requirements, distribution restrictions, advertising controls, price restrictions, or antitrust regulations -- which impact a newspaper publisher as much, if not more, than direct censorship.[258] The Austrian economist Ludwig Von Mises warned of the inherent danger in bifurcating liberties into economic and noneconomic categories:

> The fallacy of this argument stems from the spurious distinction between two realms of human life and action, entirely separated from one another, viz., the 'economic' sphere and the 'noneconomic' sphere . . . .
>
> . . .
>
> . . . as soon as the economic freedom which the market economy grants to its members is removed, all political liberties and bills of rights become humbug. Freedom of the press is a mere blind if the authority controls all printing offices and paper plants. And so are all the other rights of men.[259]

Thus, the exercise of speech may be impaired not only by the formal censorship of speech itself, but by increasing the cost of exercising that speech.[260] Alluding to occupational licensing schemes, Professor McCloskey notes that "Mark Twain would surely have felt constrained in the most fundamental sense, if his youthful aspiration to be a river-boat pilot had been

---

255 *See supra* Part IV.

256 *See supra* Parts III-IV. *Cf.* MARY ANN T. GLENDON, THE IMPOVERISHMENT OF POLITICAL DISCOURSE 24-25 (1991) (arguing that an emphasis on individual rights hampers women's achievement of economic rights).

257 See, e.g., Richard A. Epstein, *Takings: Of Maginot Lines and Constitutional Compromises*, in LIBERTY, PROPERTY, AND THE FUTURE OF CONSTITUTIONAL DEVELOPMENT 173 (Ellen Frankel Paul & Howard Dickman, eds, SUNY, 1990).

258 ROTHBARD, *supra* note 241.

259 VON MISES, *supra* note 233, at 285, 287.

260 *See id.*

frustrated by a State-ordained system of nepotism."[261] Professor McCloskey's analogy illustrates that this "cost" imposed on expression is not always a financial burden; it may easily be a personal burden that one is forced to suffer in the name of economic regulation.

B. *Solution: Protect Our Body Of Rights As A Whole*

Given the interconnected nature of rights, courts should strive to analyze legislation under a more holistic view of our entire body of rights, considering possible effects on both economic and individual spheres. If reluctant to abandon this dubious distinction in its entirety, courts should, in the first instance, account for potential collateral consequences when determining whether legislative action is "rational."[262] The body politic should also realize that valuing all constitutional rights consistently would only strengthen protections for the rights one holds most dear.

Ideally, courts should abandon the fictional distinction between individual and economic rights and recognize that both are equally important constitutional rights.[263] Courts, however, may find lukewarm the idea of weaning themselves from the individual/economic rights cleavage. Either for convenience or for fear of being themselves subject to an ill-fitting label, such as judicial activist, courts will likely continue labeling and adjudicating rights according to this suspect nomenclature. If loathe to upset almost a century of precedent, a court may, at the very least, find additional grounds for striking down already offensive legislation by setting forth a comprehensive account of all interests at stake. When reviewing economic regulation for rationality, a court may inventory the many important interests at stake, such as those of the producer, the consumer, and the individual. As exemplified by the *Meyer* Court, a holistic view of rights, including both economic and individual, would provide meaningful protection for both on an intellectually honest foundation. Such an approach, at a minimum, may transform the rational basis test into a meaningful standard of review. With a complete accounting of affected interests, a court may find that many legislative actions are not even rationally related to their purported government interests.

The body politic should also take heed of the collateral, unintended consequences of advocating deference to the legislature for laws affecting

261 *See*, Robert G. McCloskey, *Economic Due Process and the Supreme Court: An Exhumation and Reburial*, 1962 SUP. CT. REV. 34, 46 (citing Kotch v. Pilot Commissioners, 330 U.S. 552 (1947) (upholding state occupational licensing law after acknowledging its allowance for nepotism)).
262 *See* Becker, *supra* note 232 (arguing that the subjugation and regulation of economic rights is never rational).
263 Siegan, *Protecting Economic Liberties*, *supra* note 9, at 473-81.

disfavored rights. As history has shown, the legislative deference one preaches may be the very standard under which one's most revered rights are summarily dismissed.[264] Only by recognizing that economic interests are no different from, and no less important than, other personal interests, can any political ideology acquire the consistency necessary to achieve its own agenda. Indeed, it may only be through equal reverence to both "economic" and "individual" rights that we can ever expect to have meaningful protection for either.

264 *See supra* Part III.

McCann on The True Cost of Economic Rights Jurisprudence

TRUTH IS TRUTH TO THE END OF RECKONING† BUT HOW TO RECKON WHERE TRUTH BE FOUND? METHODOLOGICAL OBSTACLES FACING THE LEGAL THEORIST IN ATTEMPTING TO EXPLICATE THE NATURE OF LAW

Donna M. Lyons[1*]

† *William Shakespeare, Measure for Measure Act V, Scene 1.*

ABSTRACT

This paper examines the methodological implications of hermeneutics for legal positivism.

Part II introduces hermeneutics as a method, and explores its relevance for analytic legal philosophy. Part III argues that legal positivism cannot maintain moral neutrality while using the hermeneutic method. Complete value neutrality is a fiction. However, theorists need not endorse a specifically *moral* position during theory construction. Nevertheless, the theorist's embedded moral position inevitably influences theory construction such that the jurisprudential picture which is thereby painted is always potentially fallible. Theories purporting to provide universal truths about the *nature* of law are fallible and thus do not provide *necessary* truths because such theories must be founded on presuppositions which are reflections of fallible intuitions. Parts IV and V propose that a theoretical analysis of folk concepts via the intuitions of the theorist cannot yield essential truths about law because the method is inherently subjective. Part IV analyses the relevance of *concepts* for philosophy, concluding that a philosophical theory which uses concepts as part of the hermeneutic method must inevitably rely on intuitions in conducting its analysis.

In Part V, the author examines the relevance of intuitions for philosophy generally, and for jurisprudence specifically. Folk intuitions are explored by the legal theorist using hermeneutics. Collective (folk) intuitions cannot explain the *nature* of the world: nothing necessarily and universally true can be claimed as a result of intuitionism, only contingent truths can be built therefrom. Furthermore, where the issue of cognitive diversity is ignored, the tendency of the legal theorist to superimpose her own intuitions onto those of her subjects

---

[1] LL.B. (Hons) Trinity College Dublin, LL.M. New York University. I would like to thank Oran Doyle, Eric Engle, Shane Glackin, James Hyland, Donal Lyons, Patricia Lyons, David Prendergast and David Walker for their patient proof reading of, and contributions to, an earlier draft of this article. I would also like to extend my gratitude to Ms. Justice Susan Denham, Christopher Gosnell, Jayne Huckerby, Judge Evan J. Wallach, the NYU LL.M. class of 2009, and my family, for their inspiration and support, both academic and otherwise, over the course of the year.

renders her results even more likely to be erroneous. Therefore, theory construction as a result of hermeneutics cannot claim to be objective. Part VI explores possible alternatives to the traditional analytic legal positivist position. The author argues that viewing law as an essentially contested concept, coupled with a pragmatic approach, is the most appropriate course for jurisprudence to take in order to maintain credibility.

In Summary the Argument is:
1) Hermeneutics is a method used by the theorist which involves understanding a social system from the perspective of the social subject.
2) A majority of legal philosophers use hermeneutics during theory construction.
3) Using hermeneutics does not mean that a philosopher must endorse a specifically moral position but it does mean that reliance on personal intuitions is inevitable.
4) Legal positivists who employ hermeneutics cannot claim to have discovered the *nature* of law because reliance on intuitions, which is inevitable, produces faulty results.
5) Rather than making false claims regarding law's nature, we, as philosophers, ought to strive to accept law as an essentially contested concept, and thereby acknowledge the limitations that are placed on our pursuit by intuitionism, but remain satisfied to choose between theories of law based on their pragmatic value.

I. INTRODUCTION

Hermeneutics has been defined as "the art or theory of interpretation, as well as a type of philosophy that starts with questions of interpretation. Originally concerned more narrowly with interpreting sacred texts, the term acquired a much broader significance in its historical development."[2]

In the context of analytic legal positivism,[3] Brian Bix notes that the methodology of social sciences, "with its emphasis on the internal aspect of rules and of law, is hermeneutic in the sense that it tries to understand a

---

[2] THE CAMBRIDGE DICTIONARY OF PHILOSOPHY 323 (Robert Audi ed., 1995).

[3] Analysis decomposes objects into their constituent elements to examine those elements and their relationships to each other, the system decomposed, and even other systems and other elements of systems. Analytic philosophy is philosophy that adopts an analytic approach as the central feature of its methodology. Analytic jurisprudence is legal philosophy that draws on the resources of analytic philosophy in attempting to understand the nature of law.

practice in a way that takes into account the way the practice is perceived by its participants."[4]

Since Hart, hermeneutic methodology, by virtue of which the legal sociologist constructs her account of law consistent with the perspectives of legal participants, has been widely taken up in jurisprudence. However, the use of hermeneutics by the analytic legal positivist school of thought has caused a great deal of controversy.

In this paper, I examine the implications of hermeneutics for legal positivism. In Part II, I will introduce hermeneutics as a method, and explore its relevance for analytic legal philosophy. In Part III, I argue that legal positivism cannot maintain moral neutrality while adopting a hermeneutic approach. I will suggest that although complete value neutrality is a fiction, theorists need not endorse a specifically *moral* position[5] during theory construction, but should instead make explicit all presuppositions on which their theory is based. Any theorist's embedded moral position influences their construction of theory such that any resulting legal theory is necessarily fallible. Therefore, theories purporting to provide necessary universal truths about the essential, i.e. inevitable *nature* of law are untenable.[6] In Parts IV and V, I continue this discussion by proposing that a theoretical analysis of folk concepts via the intuitions of the theorist cannot yield essential truths about law because that method is inherently subjective.[7] In Part IV, I analyse the relevance of *concepts* for philosophy, as well as the entrenched controversy which surrounds them. I conclude that a theory which uses concepts as part of the hermeneutic method must rely on intuitions in conducting its analysis and thus, likewise, is fallible. In Part V, I will examine the relevance of intuitions for philosophy generally, and for jurisprudence specifically. Folk intuitions (i.e. collective intuitions) explored by the legal theorist using hermeneutics cannot explain the *nature* of the world. That is, nothing universally (i.e. *necessarily*) true can be claimed as a result of intuitionism. Furthermore, where the issue of cognitive diversity is ignored, the tendency of the theorist to superimpose her intuitions onto those of her subjects amplifies the already inherent fallibility of theories based on intuitions. Therefore, theory construction as a result of hermeneutics cannot claim to be objective because hermeneutics ultimately relies on (fallible)

---

4 BRIAN BIX, *H.L.A. Hart and the Hermeneutic Turn in Legal Theory* 52 S.M.U. L. REV. 167, 176 (1999). It is these broad definitions of "hermeneutics" and "hermeneutic methodology" which I will adopt in the current article.

5 According to the CAMBRIDGE DICTIONARY OF PHILOSOPHY, morality is "an informal public system applying to all rational persons, governing behaviour that affects others, having the lessening of evil or harm as its goal."

6 According to the CHAMBERS DICTIONARY, an entity's nature consists of those qualities "which make it what it is, governing its character and behaviour."

7 An intuition is the process of the mind by which it immediately perceives things without reasoning or analysis.

intuitions. As a result of the foregoing discussion, Part VI explores possible alternatives to the traditional analytic legal positivist position. I will argue that viewing law as an essentially contested concept, coupled with a pragmatic approach, is the most appropriate course for jurisprudence to take in order to maintain credibility.

II. METHODOLOGY IN THE SOCIAL SCIENCES

A. An Introduction to the Hermeneutic Method

The methodology of the social sciences differs from that of the natural sciences in important respects. Natural science is an inquiry into entities which are mind-independent and often complex. Thus, the objects of natural science are ordinarily not readily accessible to the layperson. Natural science reveals authoritative truths about the objects in question, and may override the ordinary conceptions of those who interact with such objects on a day-to-day basis. On the other hand, the social sciences generally restrict themselves to an examination of concepts with which the laity is familiar. That is, the *concepts* which are harboured by the subjects of social science are the central focus of the inquiry.[8] A successful theory of a social practice will generally ring true with the layperson, striking him as something s/he already knew, because it is *his or her own concept* which is ultimately being uncovered and explained.

Social sciences focus on social subjects (and their concepts) because of the general belief that individuals are ordinarily the best candidates for understanding the operation of their own minds. Due to the fact that social phenomena are *ipso facto* social creations, their features may be uncovered by understanding how those privy to the phenomenon collectively conceive of it.[9] A certain affinity between theorist and subject is therefore advisable:[10] because social concepts are mind-dependent, the theorist must describe and analyse them, at least in part, as understood from the subject's point of view in order to be certain that it is the subject's conception of the entity, rather than the theorist's, which is truly under investigation. Habermas summarizes the position well:

---

8 Weber is a strong advocate of this approach. *See generally* MAX WEBER, THE METHODOLOGY OF THE SOCIAL SCIENCES (1949).

9 Searle forges a useful distinction between *brute facts*, which are facts about the natural world and which exist independently of the mind, and *social facts*, which depend for their existence on human thought. The latter would include legal concepts such as rule, authority, justice, and so forth, because these concepts require human consciousness and intentionality for their creation and continuity. *See* JOHN R. SEARLE, THE CONSTRUCTION OF SOCIAL REALITY (1995).

10 That entity which is subject to examination or interpretation by the theorist.

> Without the view of law as an empirical action system, philosophical concepts remain empty. However, insofar as the sociology of law insists on an objectivating view from the outside, remaining insensitive to the symbolic dimension whose meaning is only internally accessible, sociological perception falls into the opposite danger of remaining blind.[11]

Weber has made important advances in this regard.[12] For Weber, because human action is purposive and meaningful, any description of such action must account for the values and ideals of social subjects. Weber is of the view that sociology "is a science concerning itself with the interpretative understanding of social action…We shall speak of 'action' insofar as the acting individual attaches a subjective meaning to his behaviour – be it overt or covert, omission or acquiescence."[13] He rejects the possibility of superimposing the methodology of the natural sciences onto the social sciences for this very reason: an analysis of values and motives – the subjective intent of the legal practitioner – is central to any adequate social scientific study. Out of this, Weber develops his method of *Verstehen*, or understanding. This approach requires the theorist to move closer to the attitude and motives of the subject by placing herself within the subject's mind. The *Verstehen* method is a hermeneutic method, in that it views the interpretation of human reasoning as central to any discussion about human practice. This requires the theorist to remain as value-free as possible; to put aside all value judgments when engaging in analysis, so that the position of *Verstehen* does not taint the relative objectivity of the analysis. Weber's is a dualist approach in this sense: it is sufficiently engaged to allow for an understanding of the motives behind human action, but sufficiently disengaged to allow for an objective assessment of cultural values. It is equally tailored both to the normative engagement and to the empirical description of the legal system.[14]

Peter Winch is also critical of any proposed link between the methodology of the natural sciences and that of the social sciences. In *The Idea of a Social Science*, he argues that the only way for a social scientist to understand a social practice is to analyse it from the viewpoint of the rules of that particular practice, which are essentially societal constructs.[15] For Winch, human behaviour can only be understood through the concepts which are central to that behaviour because an external analysis would inevitably

---

[11] JÜRGEN HABERMAS, BETWEEN FACTS AND NORMS 66 (1996).

[12] *See* MAX WEBER, THE METHODOLOGY OF THE SOCIAL SCIENCES (1949).

[13] MAX WEBER, ECONOMY AND SOCIETY: AN OUTLINE OF INTERPRETIVE SOCIOLOGY 4 (1978).

[14] According to the OXFORD COMPANION TO PHILOSOPHY, "normative" is the adjective derived from the noun "norm," which signifies…a standard, rule, principle used to judge or direct human conduct as something to be complied with."

[15] PETER WINCH, THE IDEA OF A SOCIAL SCIENCE (1958).

misconstrue human action.[16] Winch denies the possibility of prediction of human behaviour, because motives and reasons do not emerge from an agreed, objectively secure source. For example, the fact that two men have the same motives and reasons for undertaking something does not mean that they will both carry out the task in the same way, or indeed, that they will carry it out at all. Conversely, two practices may appear to be the same from the observer's perspective, but in fact differ widely from the participant's point of view.

For example, the practice of baptism is common to many cultures but does not always symbolize the eradication of original sin. One can argue that baptism thus has a deeper, more fundamental meaning which can be rationalized from an external vantage point, or, one can take the more satisfactory approach of examining each practice in light of the motivations of those involved, allowing that there may be practices which appear to be the same, but which in fact differ widely.[17] Trying to explicate a *deeper* meaning from what seem to be common practices as between different cultures is, in my opinion, a meaningless expedition. The practice of baptism may appear to be the same as between different cultures, but what is truly being performed can only adequately be understood where the social scientist is directly engaged with the thoughts and motivations behind the practice. When the subject under examination is physical, according to Winch, the criteria for reference as to what is the *same* or *different* are available to the observer. On the other hand:

> [W]hen one is dealing with intellectual (or indeed any kind of social) "things", that is not so. For their *being* intellectual or social, as opposed to physical, in character depends entirely on their belonging in a certain way to a system of ideas or mode of life…It follows that if the sociological investigator wants to regard them *as* social events…he has to take seriously the criteria which are applied for distinguishing…within the way of life he is studying. It is not open to him arbitrarily to impose his own standards from without. In so far as he does so, the events he is studying lose altogether their character as *social* events.[18]

This methodological advance has had far-reaching effects in the social sciences, and its influence in the jurisprudential sphere has been felt in no

16 *Id.* at 83-84.

17 Pareto argues that baptism should be examined from the point of view of the observer, revealing deeper and more fundamental truths about the practice, rather than explicating its content via the self-understandings of those internal to the system. *See* VILFREDO PARETO, THE MIND AND SOCIETY (1935).

18 WINCH, *supra* at 108. Emphasis original.

small way. I will examine the philosophy of law in light of this development before analysing the criticisms which have arisen out of its formulation.

B. The Initiation of Hermeneutics in the Jurisprudential Arena

Hart was the first well known contemporary jurisprudent to model his theory of law on a hermeneutic foundation. *The Concept of Law* is a self-proclaimed essay in "descriptive sociology."[19] Hart's philosophy is both descriptive and analytic and his project began as a critical response to the Austinian conception of law as orders backed by threats of sanction, as "key to the science of jurisprudence".[20] Austin reduces all of law to commands of the sovereign, a conclusion which leads him to adopt a scientific and therefore predictive approach. As a result of this, Austin cannot capture the meaning of (purely theoretical) concepts which are exclusively internal to the practice of law, since predicting human behaviour based on scientific models will lead to inaccurate results.[21] For Hart, a descriptive account which proceeds from an external perspective such as Austin's cannot successfully capture much of what occurs in legal life: it is value-free, but it lacks descriptive depth.[22]

Per Hart: if the theorist defers to the views of legal participants, rather than making judgments which are external to the social practice, she will be in a better position to select what is important and significant about that practice, and thereby have a foothold from which to construct her theory of law. From his position of understanding how others understand themselves, Hart concludes that normativity in general, and primary and secondary rules in particular, are of prime importance to the actors within any legal system.[23]

Austin was blind to this fact because he maintained an external perspective, whereby the spectator can note nothing more than the observable regularities of conduct of legal participants. By Hart's lights, "[f]or such an observer, deviations by a member of the group from normal conduct will be a sign that

---

[19] H.L.A. HART, THE CONCEPT OF LAW § Preface (2d ed. 1994).

[20] JOHN AUSTIN, THE PROVINCE OF JURISPRUDENCE DETERMINED Lecture I, 13 (Weidenfeld and Nicolsan eds., 1968).

[21] For example, Austin would posit that legal subjects are inclined to stop at traffic lights on the basis that they will be sanctioned should they not do so. However, as an examination of the internal perspective highlights, individuals will stop at traffic lights for a variety of reasons, for example, the desire one might have to lead life according to normative rules, and thus the preceding account of human behaviour at traffic lights would be inaccurate.

[22] According to Hart, "For the understanding of [law] the methodology of the empirical sciences is useless; what is needed is a 'hermeneutic' method which involves portraying rule-governed behaviour as it appears to its participants…" H.L.A. HART, ESSAYS IN JURISPRUDENCE AND PHILOSOPHY, 13 (1983).

[23] For a discussion of primary and secondary rules leading to the normativity of which Hart speaks, *see* H.L.A. HART, THE CONCEPT OF LAW, *supra*, at 91-99.

hostile reaction is likely to follow, and nothing more."[24] The concept of law is a concept which is understood and frequently used by the participants of a legal system. For Hart, therefore, the theorist who views the law from within gains a deeper understanding of the practice:

> What the external point of view...cannot reproduce is the way in which the rules function as rules in the lives of those who normally are the majority of society...For them the violation of a rule is not merely a basis for the prediction that a hostile reaction will follow but a *reason* for hostility.[25]

Like Weber, Hart's approach is dualist. He is interested in engaging with the motives and values of legal participants, but is nevertheless acutely aware of the necessity of remaining sufficiently disengaged from the practice in order to provide a relatively objective portrayal of the legal system.

Shapiro suggests that Hart's focus on critical reflection forges an indissoluble bond between the hermeneutic perspective and the perspective of the law-abiding citizen.[26] That is, rather than advocating a *general* hermeneutic approach to jurisprudence, Hart is emphasizing the indispensability of the *law-abiding* perspective in any theory of law. After all, Hart's criticism of Holmes would not succeed if he were merely advocating a general hermeneutic jurisprudence. Hart's dissatisfaction with Holmes' theory of law, as investigated from the perspective of the "bad man," centers on the fact that such an explanation is incoherent: it cannot itself account for the sanctions which the bad man is trying to avoid. General hermeneutics *would* allow the "bad man" theory to stand because Holmes' bad man is unmistakably a *participant* in the legal system: he is simply a participant who does not possess the practical attitude of rule acceptance. Therefore, Hart's conception of the internal perspective appears to be narrower than a simple vindication of the hermeneutic method.

This suggestion strikes a chord, particularly when we note Hart's dismissal of the non-law-abiding perspective as nothing more than an "external" perspective on law. However, rather than arbitrarily selecting this attitude of rule acceptance, Hart is choosing the perspective which best explains the

---

24 HART, *id.* at 90.

25 *Id.* Emphasis original.

26 *See generally* SCOTT SHAPIRO, *What is the Internal Point of View?*, 75 FORDHAM L. REV. 1157 (2006-2007). *See also* SCOTT SHAPIRO, *On Hart's Way Out*, 4 LEGAL THEORY 469 (1998); SCOTT SHAPIRO, *Law, Morality and the Guidance of Conduct*, 6 LEGAL THEORY 127 (2000). Jules Coleman agrees with this analysis. *See* JULES COLEMAN, *Methodology*, *in* COLEMAN & SHAPIRO eds., THE OXFORD HANDBOOK OF JURISPRUDENCE AND PHILOSOPHY OF LAW 339-340, fn. 38 (2004). For an earlier version of this material, *see* JULES COLEMAN, THE PRACTICE OF PRINCIPLE 179-217 (2001).

features of law which are intuitive to those living under the system, features on which there exists consensus,[27] such as norms, sanctions, dispute resolution, and so on. Insofar as the law-abiding citizen elucidates these features in a coherent fashion, it is the perspective to be preferred. Theories of law constructed from the bad man's perspective, focussing narrowly on sanctions, cannot account for the very existence of sanctions: if all citizens obeyed the law for fear of sanction, a circular account of law would ensue. There would be no means by which we could explain a judge's or a legislator's behaviour in creating law; to argue that law is created for fear of sanction arising out of that very law is an interminable and incoherent argument.

Further, theories focussing narrowly on adjudication vis-à-vis the perspective of the judge cannot explain the normative nature of law in everyday life.[28] For Hart, the law-abiding citizen, considering law as a system of primary and secondary rules, provides the most coherent account of what we intuitively consider the many facets of law.

Despite this narrow view, Hart remains a staunch defender of hermeneutics as a central part of the jurisprudential endeavour.[29] It is this general approach which allows him to *locate* the features which are significant and important about law and therefore which leads him to select one perspective over another. Without general hermeneutics, this process would not have been possible to begin with.

Hermeneutics has been an important feature of legal sociology since Hart. There has been widespread consensus on its worth for a social scientific analysis of law, particularly within analytic legal philosophy. Indeed, Postema notes that "virtually unchallenged is the view that jurisprudence is fundamentally interpretative or 'hermeneutic.'"[30] Nevertheless, a number of controversies have arisen as a direct result of this methodological development. Notable among these is the question whether and how value neutrality in theory construction is even possible. I will now turn to this debate.

---

[27] I will outline in Part V of this paper that assumptions of consensus and cognitive uniformity by the theorist will often amount to theoretical fictions. For the moment it is adequate to note that this is generally what the theorist considers herself to be doing.

[28] Ronald Dworkin's theory of law is an appropriate example in this context of a theory of law focussing on the internal perspective of adjudicators rather than citizens.

[29] *See generally* H.L.A. HART, ESSAYS IN JURISPRUDENCE AND PHILOSOPHY 13 (1983). *See also* BRIAN BIX, *H.L.A. Hart and the Hermeneutic Turn in Legal Theory* 52 S.M.U. L. REV. 167 (1999) (for a discussion of the role played by Hart in legal theory's hermeneutic shift).

[30] GERALD POSTEMA, *Jurisprudence as Practical Philosophy* 4 LEGAL THEORY 329, 329 (1998). Postema points out that one notable exception to this trend is the philosophy of Michael Moore.

III. A DEFENCE OF MORAL NEUTRALITY

Due to the general commitment by many legal philosophers to hermeneutics, questions have been posed as to the continuing possibility of value neutrality within analytic legal positivism. If the theorist chooses to examine the concept of law from the perspective of the legal participant, to what extent can she remain morally neutral in explicating the content of the concept? I argue that hermeneutics does not require the jurisprudent to commit herself to a given moral position in order to describe the concept of law. However, I argue that complete value neutrality is impossible and therefore the legal theorist who wishes to objectively discover the nature of law will face substantial difficulties. One of the central tasks of legal positivism is to provide a theory of law which describes the legal system as it *is* in a value neutral manner - separate from theories of law seeking to provide guidance on how the system *ought* to function – partly in order to overcome some of the difficulties in discovering what law is. Austin describes the position as such:

> The existence of the law is one thing; its merit or demerit is another. Whether it be or be not is one enquiry; whether it be or be not conformable to an assumed standard, is another enquiry. A law, which actually exists, is a law, though we happen to dislike it, or though it vary from the text, by which we regulate our approbation and disapprobation.[31]

There are two arguments for the position that a hermeneutic approach to jurisprudence undermines this claim to value neutrality. The first is proposed by Finnis, and slightly differently by Perry, and is based on the fact that the selection which is made by the theorist between internal perspectives in describing the law is a moral choice. The second attack is posed by Dworkin, and is echoed by Oberdiek and Patterson, who argue that all interpretation is value-laden and that interpretation of a normative practice must therefore be normative. I will examine the merits and flaws of both positions below.

A. Moral Neutrality in Theory Construction Is Possible

Finnis is acutely aware of the methodological difficulties facing legal philosophy. He notes that descriptive theorists arrive at different theories of the legal system, despite the fact that they each analyse the same data:

> It is obvious, then, that the differences in description derive from differences of opinion, amongst the descriptive theorists, about what is

---

[31] AUSTIN, *supra*, at 184.

> *important* and *significant* in the field of data and experience with which they are all equally and thoroughly familiar.[32]

Finnis agrees that hermeneutics is the only method by which one can truly understand law.[33] However, internal perspectives in law are generally normative in nature. Participants view their own behaviour in a moral light: they *ought* to respect authority, they *should* obey the law, they *have a moral obligation* to respect the rights of others, and so on. According to Finnis, therefore, in selecting one perspective over another, it is difficult for the theorist to justify her choice except on moral grounds. Theorists, rather than selecting a perspective arbitrarily, should select it according to the tenets of practical reasonableness, that is, by "understanding what is really good for human persons…"[34] For Finnis, then, the theorist has no option but to incorporate moral argument into her exposition of the legal system.
Perry does not stand far from Finnis on this issue. Perry makes the argument that:

> Jurisprudence requires a conceptual framework. The difficulty is that the data can plausibly be conceptualized in more than one way, and choosing among conceptualizations seems to require the attribution to law of a point or function. This in turn involves not just evaluative considerations, but also moral argument.[35]

The objective of philosophy, for Perry, is to clarify the way we conceptualize our practice. Therefore, in order to explain why a citizen respects a legal authority, the theorist must portray the respectability of the authority, thereby, "showing that it is justified."[36] Perry thus interprets Hart as saying that law is morally justified because it is capable of guiding conduct in a way that is socially beneficial. In short, if there are two competing accounts of the legal material, Perry is of the view that the theorist must choose between them on moral grounds.

---

[32] JOHN FINNIS, NATURAL LAW AND NATURAL RIGHTS 9 (1980). Emphasis original.

[33] Finnis notes that the theorist must "assess importance or significance in similarities and differences within his subject-matter by asking what would be considered important or significant in that field by those whose concerns, decisions, and activities create or constitute the subject-matter." John FINNIS, NATURAL LAW AND NATURAL RIGHTS,12 (Oxford: Clarendon Press, 1980).

[34] *Id.* at 3.

[35] STEPHEN PERRY, *Interpretation and Methodology in Legal Theory*, *in* Andrei Marmor eds., LAW AND INTERPRETATION 123 (1997).

[36] STEPHEN PERRY, *Hart's Methodological Positivism*, *in* Jules Coleman eds., HART'S POSTSCRIPT: ESSAYS ON THE POSTSCRIPT TO THE CONCEPT OF LAW 347 (2001). *See also* STEPHEN PERRY, *Holmes v. Hart: the Bad Man in Legal Theory*, *in* THE PATH OF LAW AND ITS INFLUENCE: THE LEGACY OF OLIVER WENDELL HOLMES JUNIOR (1988); STEPHEN PERRY, *Hart on Social Rules and the Foundation of Law: Liberating the Internal Point of View* 75 FORDHAM L. REV. 1171 (2006).

There is no doubt that competing accounts of the positive material will arise. To borrow Nietzsche's words, it is possible "to conceive a reality that can be resolved into a plurality of fictions relative to multiple standpoints."[37] I will use an example to demonstrate this point. Take the concept of war: war is a social practice which is understood by participants in many different ways. For instance, one set of participants might equate the practice with the morally bankrupt, meaningless destruction of life and property, which ought to be avoided at all costs. Another set of participants might view it as a morally necessary method of dispute resolution, resulting in the protection of basic human values. Both conceptualizations are plausible. Due to the fact that both are also moral in nature, Perry would argue that selection of one over the other can be nothing more than an intuitive agreement with one camp, and is thus a selection based on morality. If the theorist views war as morally necessary through the attitude of the second internal perspective, by Perry's lights, she must show how the necessity of war is justified according to her basic moral values.

Ultimately, this argument is not supportable. Finnis and Perry make a sound argument to the effect that a choice as between competing normative conceptualizations of the practice must be made. However, they do not explain why it is only *normative* conceptualizations which are competing: the *external* attitude, that is, the citizen who views law in a predictive manner, can still provide a description of law, even if that description captures less of what we consider the intuitive features of law.

Furthermore, Finnis is correct to note that evaluation as to what is *significant* and *important* about the subject matter under examination must be made. However, requiring that such evaluation be moral in nature is an unnecessary logical leap: it is certainly *possible* to make the choice based on moral considerations, but it is also possible to decide *without* referring to such considerations.

Leiter's distinction between epistemic and moral values is useful in this context.[38] For Leiter, epistemic values outline the "truth-conducive desiderata" in theory construction, values such as "evidentiary adequacy, simplicity, minimum mutilation of well-established theoretical frameworks and methods…, explanatory consilience, and so forth."[39] Conversely, moral values

---

37 FRIEDRICH NIETZSCHE, as cited by Mary Hesse. *See* MARY HESSE, *Habermas' Consensus Theory of Truth* 2 PROCEEDINGS OF THE BIENNIAL MEETING OF THE PHILOSOPHY OF SCIENCE ASSOCIATION 373, 375 (1978).

38 BRIAN LEITER, *Beyond the Hart/Dworkin Debate: The Methodology Problem in Jurisprudence* 48 AM. J. JURIS. 17, 34-35 (2003).

39 *Id.* Perry also makes reference to such meta-theoretical criteria, providing the examples of a theory's "predictive power, coherence, range of phenomena explained, degree of

determine how one ought to live one's life as a matter of practical reasonableness, and are not a necessary element of the descriptive process. The distinction is critical because epistemic values allow the theorist to select one theoretical description over another without sacrificing moral neutrality.

In relation to the example of war provided above, the promise of theoretical consistency as a meta-theoretical or epistemic value may allow the theorist to choose the second conceptualization of the practice – the attitude that war is a morally necessary practice – as the more accurate one. As noted above, the theorist selects the features of law which she believes to be relevant to those participating in the legal system.[40] To the extent that her intuition coincides with that of those internal to the system, the feature of law will be retained as part of the theory. If there is widespread disagreement among participants as to which features are relevant, the theorist will have to prioritize aspects on her own terms. However, even this measure does not require her to make moral choices. Choices as to significance will be defined by a person's history and system of belief, much of which contains moral content. This is precisely why different people can arrive at different theories of a social practice based on the same material evidence. However, while values are never entirely separate from the critical process, a choice as to significance does not automatically become a positive endorsement. Indeed, our value system will often lead us to choose aspects of the material which are morally repugnant as significant for this very reason. For many of us, murder is a significant feature of the Nazi system because it stands out as important; and it strikes us as important because we understand it to have a crucially negative effect on society. In many ways, the terms 'value' and 'morality' are ambiguous: complete value-freedom is impossible. However, Perry and Finnis go too far: they argue that morality in the form of practical reasoning must be involved. Ultimately, a choice as to significance, while aided by the embedded moral perspective of the theorist, is not equivalent to practical reasoning: it by no means represents endorsement or justification of the practice under surveillance. Perhaps choices as to significance and positive endorsements can be placed at ends of the same scale, but they nevertheless lie at *opposite* ends of that scale, to the extent that it would be wrong to equate them when criticizing a theory of law.

Once the relevant features of the system are chosen, they are then collated, and the internal perspective which best elucidates these generally agreed features is prioritized. The first account of war above could be criticized on

explanatory unity, and the theory's simplicity or elegance." *See* STEPHEN PERRY, *Hart's Methodological Positivism*, *supra*, at 314.

[40] Description of a normative attitude may be done in a value-free way, an argument which I will explore in more detail in Section B. This particular argument turns on the possibility of *selecting* one moral position over another.

the basis that meaningless destruction does not account for the fact that war is often a highly organized, strategically sophisticated endeavour. Whichever perspective has the potential to yield a theoretically consistent account is the perspective to be prioritized. It should be noted that this is a moot point: one could validly argue for either of the perspectives in the war debate, but the persuasiveness of the theory will rest on its intuitive correctness. Whether or not the perspective is morally preferable, it is selected primarily on meta-theoretical grounds. There is no doubting that meta-theoretical considerations are still value-laden: determining what constitutes a *good* description requires evaluative reflection. Personal values are likely to color any type of selection, be it selection as to importance and significance, or selection as to which epistemic values are to be prioritized in theory construction. However, this is a very different evaluative process to one which results in the endorsement or otherwise of the practice under examination. Deciding which conceptualization fits more comfortably with the practice under observation lies worlds apart from deciding which conceptualization of the practice is *morally* preferable. It is high time for legal theory to take heed of this distinction, in order to allow the debate to move forward.

I will now turn to the critique which is presented against legal positivism on the basis that the interpretative nature of human thought does not admit of moral neutrality in theory construction.

B. Moral Neutrality in the Interpretation of a Normative Practice is Possible

Dworkin is one of positivism's most persistent critics.[41] He insists on the interpretative nature of law and legal theory. In order to understand law, Dworkin argues, one must recognize its purpose, and therefore harbour a political justification for it. For Dworkin:

> General theories of law…are constructive interpretations: they try to show legal practice as a whole in its best light, to achieve equilibrium between legal practice as they find it and the best justification of that practice.[42]

According to Dworkin, the purpose of law is justification of state coercion and thus any explanation of the law must be justificatory.[43] The ascription of

41 *See generally* RONALD DWORKIN, *The Model of Rules* 35 UNI. CHICAGO L. REV. 14 (1967); RONALD DWORKIN, *Hard Cases* 88 HARV. L. REV. 1057 (1975); RONALD DWORKIN, LAW'S EMPIRE (1986).

42 DWORKIN, LAW'S EMPIRE, *supra*, at 90.

43 Dworkin notes that "[l]aw insists that force not be used or withheld, no matter how useful that would be to ends in view, no matter how beneficial or noble these ends, except as license or required by individual rights and responsibilities flowing from past political decisions about when collective force is justified." Dworkin, LAW'S EMPIRE, *supra*, at 93.

this purpose to law is generally accepted as intuitively incorrect, and primarily results from the fact that Dworkin, without justification, prioritizes the perspective of the judiciary in his account of law. Legal philosophy, for him, is not dissimilar to adjudication, since both activities entail the presentation of positive material in its best light.

However, jurisprudence is much more than merely adjudication. Adjudication is concerned primarily with the positive materials in identifying *the law*. Legal sociology, on the other hand, is primarily concerned with providing an account of law as a whole, including (especially) the behaviour of citizens in relation to *law*. This distinction, which was apparently overlooked by Dworkin, is a critical one because it determines the scope and effect of the material under examination.

Whereas judges generally *do* perceive the law in a purposive and justificatory manner, citizens often view it in terms of its regulatory effect. For many citizens it is a method of social guidance rather than a predictive game of sanction-avoidance. Raz correctly believes that Dworkin's philosophy of law is:

> [A] theory of adjudication rather than a theory of (the nature of) law. Dworkin's failure to allow that the two are not the same is one reason for the failure of his conception of the tasks and method of jurisprudence.[44]

Furthermore, it is clear that neither adjudication nor legal theory always strives to present data in its best light.[45] For Dworkin, the more justified the theory of law, the more true it is, and therefore what law *ought to be* is ultimately what it *is*.[46] He forges no distinction between the actual and the desirable.

However, equating what is and what ought be is an error: there are countless cases where the participant's desired conception of law differs from the reality of the legal system. Ofer Raban cogently argues against the possibility of equating desirability with truth.[47] He soundly argues that:

---

[44] JOSEPH RAZ, *Two Views on the Nature of the Theory of Law: A Partial Comparison*, *in* Coleman eds., HART'S POSTSCRIPT, *supra*, at 37.

[45] For a general refutation of Dworkin's "best light" requirement, see ANDREI MARMOR, INTERPRETATION AND LEGAL THEORY Chapter 3 (2d ed., 2005).

[46] This is a logical follow-on the notion that law is justified state coercion: if, according to Dworkin, this is the case, then unjustified state coercion is not law. Therefore, this amounts to equating what *is* and what *ought* to be.

[47] OFER RABAN, *Dworkin's 'Best Light' Requirement and the Proper Methodology of Legal Theory* 23 OXFORD J. LEG. STUD. 243 (2003).

> An interpretation may claim to be the most desirable conception of law without also claiming to be a true conception…And, obviously, an interpretation may claim to be a true conception of law without being the most desirable.[48]

Dworkin criticizes positivism on the ground that it maintains a strict division between the interpreter and the legal material. Dworkin disregards this fact-value distinction: for Dworkin the role of the philosopher is to reconstruct the meaning embodied in the positive material. Interpreting a practice and justifying it become the same process, and therefore personal morality is essential to the discovery of meaning.[49] While one of Dworkin's greatest contributions to legal philosophy is his argument for the evaluative nature of interpretation, the relationship which he forms between interpretation and justification is untenable.[50]

Before exploring this argument in more detail, it is important to note that Oberdiek and Patterson make a similar claim.[51] They argue that all interpretation requires some amount of evaluation and thus any interpretation of a moral entity is necessarily a moral investigation. For them, the rule of law is specifically moral in nature, and therefore moral argument is necessary to explicate its content.[52] They claim that "[t]he rule of law always adds something of value to the societies that possess it"[53] and that "the formal fairness demanded by the rule of law expresses a view about the moral status of a people, namely, that persons are worthy of being treated in non-arbitrary ways."[54] This argument takes a different angle to Perry and Finnis, who were sceptical of the possibility of value neutral *selection*. Instead, Oberdiek and Patterson, like Dworkin, take issue with the possibility of neutrally describing a normative concept at all. However, this argument is flawed in two ways. Firstly, the fact that there is moral merit inherent in the rule of law is contestable. Secondly, and more importantly, even if the rule of law adds something of value to society, it can nevertheless be described without being morally endorsed or rejected.

---

48 *Id.* at 259.

49 I have argued elsewhere that this proposition stands in direct conflict with Dworkin's argument for the pre-existence of law. *See generally* DONNA LYONS, *Dworkin and Judicial Discretion: A Critical Analysis of the Pre-Existence Thesis* 11 T.C.L.R. 1 (2008).

50 Dworkin suggests that the theorist should impose a "purpose on an object or practice in order to make of it the best possible example of the form or genre to which it is taken to belong." Dworkin, LAW'S EMPIRE, *supra, at* 52.

51 JOHN OBERDIEK & DENNIS PATTERSON, *Moral Evaluation and Conceptual Analysis in Jurisprudential Methodology*, *in* Ross Harrison eds., CURRENT LEGAL ISSUES: LAW AND PHILOSOPHY (2007).

52 Oberdiek & Patterson argue, for these purposes, that the rule of law is central to the concept of law.

53 OBERDIEK & PATTERSON, *supra*, at 12-13.

54 *Id.* at 14.

I will analyse this latter point in refuting both Dworkin and Oberdiek and Patterson. Before doing so, it must be conceded that theory construction is never *entirely* presumptionless.

Popper's view is instructive in this regard.[55] According to Popper, the scientific endeavor does not begin with observations and subsequently infer a general theory based on those observations. Instead, scientists propose a theory and then compare its predictions with observations about the physical world, attempting to uncover whether the original theory withstands the positive evidence. If the theory fails in this regard, it is *falsified*. On the other hand, if the evidence squares with the theory, the latter is retained, not as proven truth, but as unrefuted hypothesis. A single refutation will prove fatal, but no amount of supporting evidence will prove the theory's truth. Therefore, Popper maintains that science is speculative: that it is not so much that we know A is true, as we know all other hypotheses are false. The only (but important) difference between science and other forms of belief is that the former is authoritatively falsifiable. This important contention was taken up by Kuhn, who argues that scientific thought is defined by paradigms, systems of belief shared by a given set of people at any moment in the history of science.[56] Paradigms are accepted methods of inquiry, yielding what is considered authoritative knowledge for those within the system of belief. However, when evidence emerges giving rise to anomalies within the paradigm, a shift is likely to occur, whereby the old paradigm is replaced by a new one, and thus a new system of thought replaces the falsified one. According to Kuhn, the paradigms are incommensurable, that is, it is impossible to compare them from within the conceptual framework of one system. Therefore, scientific thought, and knowledge in general, is not authoritatively true, but rather, based on presumptions which alter considerably over time.

Legal theory, in this sense, requires that theorists have certain presumptions when embarking on theory construction. A theorist must select features of the legal system which she considers significant and important. She must adhere to the epistemic values of theory construction. She must decide which aspects of law require explanation and which do not. Some amount of evaluation is a *sine qua non* of legal theory: if selection were not possible, descriptions would be lengthy, incoherent, unworkable and largely futile. Dickson correctly notes that jurisprudence:

---

55 KARL POPPER, THE LOGIC OF SCIENTIFIC DISCOVERY (2d ed., 1968). *See also*, KARL POPPER, ALL LIFE IS PROBLEM SOLVING (1999) (for the expression and expansion of these and similar views). For a critical exposition of Popper's thought, see A.F. CHALMERS, WHAT IS THIS THING CALLED SCIENCE? (3d ed., 1999).

56 THOMAS KUHN, THE STRUCTURE OF SCIENTIFIC REVOLUTIONS (3d ed., 1996).

> [D]oes much more than merely report on the views about the law held by those subject to it, attempting as it does to systematise, clarify, sieve for importance and relevance and incorporate them into a cogent and persuasive account of the nature of law.[57]

However, as I will go on to discuss below, while theory construction is inevitably value-laden, it does not require the theorist to *endorse* the values under investigation. Our interpretation of a value requires us to have an understanding of that value, but it is possible to describe the value in a manner which does not constitute an express endorsement or rejection of it. In short, an understanding of self-conception does not lead to value-complicity. Coleman is correct in claiming that a characterization of the self-conception of legal participants would emphasize the characteristic of law as justification-centered.[58] However, while we must take into account the justificatory manner in which citizens conceive of their own behaviour, "this does not mean that we must *credit* those self-understandings in the context of trying to understand what the practice is."[59]

I will use a second example to demonstrate this critique. The Mafia wields authority through the vigorous exercise of violence. For those operating within the Mafia system, the organization is not criminal, but rather, acts as a role model and as a protective force in society. The Mafiosi are considered 'men of honor' and the omertà is the code by which they operate. This is the Code of Honor. The Code maintains that justice, honor and vengeance fall within the realm of men and not the state. Honor requires that secrecy of, and respect for, the Mafia be preserved through silence, and that a breach of the Code of Honor will incur retribution from the organization. The Mafia thus constitutes a normative social system with the value of honor at its very core. Let us, for the purposes of this example, presume that honor is a moral concept and that it adds value to the society in which it operates, according to those within its scope: in this case, the community ruled by the Mafia. Does this mean that a description of its content cannot be undertaken without employing moral argument? There is a certain level of understanding that is undoubtedly required: the theorist must understand what it is to feel honor, and to live according to its tenets. Somebody who has never encountered the concept will admittedly be unable to carry out an accurate description of it – that person will only be able to observe regularities of behaviour in an Austinian sense, resulting in a rather thin description of the practice. However, the person who does *understand* what it means to feel honor will be in an appropriate position to describe the value. The observer must also be able to

57 JULIE DICKSON, EVALUATION AND LEGAL THEORY 43 (2001).
58 COLEMAN, METHODOLOGY, *supra*, at 324.
59 *Id.* at 326.

understand that the value has a moral aspect: this recognition is essential to understanding the pivotal role that it plays in such a society. Nevertheless, it does not require the observer to endorse the moral aspect.[60] Using Raz's concept of the detached legal statement, we can understand and describe the viewpoint accurately without any endorsement or rejection of its moral merit.[61] In Raz's terms, the meat-eater can quite effortlessly inform the vegetarian that she should not eat a meat-based broth, whether or not the former agrees with the philosophy of vegetarianism.[62] The meat-eater need only understand the value of vegetarianism in the abstract: she need not find it an appealing moral position. Therefore, the observer may have to understand the purpose or point of the practice, but this does not lead to the requirement that a moral justification for this point is provided. In the Mafia context, one might find the Code of Honor utterly reprehensible, but still be capable of describing its relative worth for those who value it. There are no comprehensively neutral descriptions, but the theorist's awareness of her role as such allows her to consciously reduce the evaluative aspect of her description. In the last analysis, if all members of the Mafia system consider the concept of honor as worthy and valuable, she is perfectly capable of referring to this fact and describing it, without assenting to it or endorsing it.

The moral neutrality debate is thus resolvable. Neither the Perry-Finnis critique, nor the Dworkin-Oberdiek-Patterson critique, undermines the possibility of morally neutral theory construction. Nevertheless, the theorist will always bring her own presumptions into the jurisprudential sphere, thereby influencing her analysis. While embedded presumptions do not necessarily constitute (moral) justification, they nevertheless render claims to objectivity fallible. The theorist who purports to yield necessary truths about the nature of law based on a presumption-laden inquiry will not withstand

---

60 Indeed, many people external to the Mafia system have strong moral objections to the concept of honour in this context. One example is Terranova, an Italian Magistrate who ruled that "[t]he myth of a courageous and generous 'man of honor' must be destroyed, because a Mafioso is just the opposite" and who, incidentally, was murdered for his words in 1979.

61 It should be noted that Raz, an exclusive legal positivist and one of the most rigorous proponents of the separation thesis in modern times, remains committed to hermeneutic methodology. He agrees that "[i]t is a major task of legal theory to advance our understanding of society by helping us understand how people understand themselves." *See* JOSEPH RAZ, ETHICS IN THE PUBLIC DOMAIN: ESSAYS IN THE MORALITY OF LAW AND POLITICS 221 (1994). Raz also agrees with Hart to the effect that "[d]escription may still be description, even when what is described is an evaluation." *See* H.L.A. HART, THE CONCEPT OF LAW, *supra*, at 244.

62 JOSEPH RAZ, PRACTICAL REASON AND NORMS 175 (1999). For other examples of this notion, see JOSEPH RAZ, THE AUTHORITY OF LAW, 156-157 (2002).

close scrutiny.[63] I will examine this in more detail below in the context of philosophical concepts and intuitions.

IV. PHILOSOPHICAL CONCEPTS

A serious challenge for the analytic legal positivist in present day jurisprudence is her defence of the claim to essentiality[64] on the basis of conceptual analysis. The commitment of the legal theorist to hermeneutics means that she is required to analyse *concepts* which are understood by participants within the social system. A scientific, predictive approach is neither appropriate nor satisfactory for this type of analysis, since social constructs are inherently changeable and unpredictable. However, if it is the folk concept which is being examined by the theorist, questions arise as to the strength of conceptual analysis as a methodology, since the theorist's presumptions will always influence her interpretation of societal concepts.

Hermeneutic analytical positivist theories of law are generally constructed thus: the theorist reflects on what she considers to be the central features of law. To the extent that such features reflect the way in which the concept of law is intuitively understood by those living under the system, these features will form part of the theory. The theorist then chooses an internal perspective in accordance with the central aspects of law in order to elucidate the concept more fully. The theory which is constructed therefrom will be more or less successful depending on its intuitive correctness to those operating within the system. This, at least, is what theorist considers herself to be doing. The reality, I will argue, is quite another matter.

To my mind, there are two important stages in this process, namely (i) the delineation of the ambit of the theory based on participant intuition, and
(ii) the success of the theory based on participant intuition. In other words, what is *significant* about law, and what ultimately makes a theory *true*,[65] are both factors which depend for their existence on the intuitions of internal participants about the concept.

---

[63] According to the OXFORD COMPANION TO PHILOSOPHY, logical necessity is that which "follows from the laws of logic alone." Necessary truth, therefore, is truth which is, by nature, necessary.

[64] According to the CAMBRIDGE DICTIONARY OF PHILOSOPHY, "[a] property is essential to an entity if, necessarily, the entity cannot exist without being an instance of the property."

[65] In reality, this denotes theory-success rather than truth. Although theorists are quick to make claims to truth based on intuition, I will argue in Part V that the possibility of such truth is in fact impossible.

What if the possibility of exploring the intuitions of participants via conceptual analysis were to fall away? Would truth based on armchair philosophy be possible?[66] I will initially review the debate surrounding concepts in current philosophy. I will subsequently conclude that reliance on intuitions remains a central aspect of the philosophical endeavor, and I will suggest that the analytic project is thereby subject to substantial criticism as a result.

A. What are Concepts?

Concepts are situated at the center of analytic jurisprudence.[67] Bix notes that "[a] concept is a category of thought by which we divide up the world."[68] Coleman also points out that "[t]he aim of Conceptual Analysis is to uncover interesting and informative truths about the concepts we employ to make the world rationally intelligible to us."[69] More specifically, the *concept* constitutes the possible situations which are referred to by a particular term.[70] However, rather than simply referring to all those instances where a word is used, (law, after all, can refer to a whole host of different entities) we distil our concept based on an implicit coherence between the terms used in a certain context. Therefore, jurisprudents recognize that there is something consistent in the way we term law in relation to the state, in contrast, for example, to the way it is used in relation to the laws of mathematics. Conceptual analysis is the method by which the theorist uncovers the properties which are common to all subjects in a given set, in order to reduce these properties to more fundamental terms.[71] For Jackson, the main defender of conceptual methodology in recent times, "conceptual analysis is the very business of

---

66 According to the CAMBRIDGE DICTIONARY OF PHILOSOPHY, truth is "the quality of those propositions that accord with reality, specifying what is in fact the case."

67 Since analytic jurisprudence is, by definition, concerned with the elucidation of legal concepts, by their very nature they lie at the center of the jurisprudential enterprise. The CAMBRIDGE DICTIONARY OF PHILOSOPHY states thus: "analytic philosophers have tried to analyse the concept of propositions. This is conceptual analysis."

68 BRIAN BIX, *Raz, Authority, and Conceptual Analysis* 50 AM. J. JURIS. 311, 315 (2005).

69 COLEMAN, *Methodology*, *supra*, at 344.

70 *See also,* CAMBRIDGE DICTIONARY OF PHILOSOPHY: "a concept may be understood as a principle of classification, something that can guide us in determining whether an entity belongs in a given class or does not...[concepts are] general words (adjectives, common nouns, verbs) or uses of such words, an entity's belonging to a certain class being determined by the applicability to the entity of the appropriate word." Schroeter also notes that "[the philosophical analyst] thinks that our implicit understanding of what it is a concept represents *determines the reference* of the concept." *See* LAURA SCHROETER, 85 *Pacific Philosophical Quarterly* 425, 426 (2004)

71 *See,* Roderiguez-Blanco notes that "[t]he goal of conceptual analysis is to describe or define concepts in terms of other concepts or perhaps to say certain things in one vocabulary in terms of a more fundamental vocabulary..." VERONICA RODERIGUEZ-BLANCO, A DEFENCE OF HART'S SEMANTICS AS NONAMBITIOUS CONCEPTUAL ANALYSIS 9 *Legal Theory*, 99, 102 (2003).

addressing when and whether a story told in one vocabulary is made true by one told in some allegedly more fundamental vocabulary."[72] Moreover, Farrell points out that "in general conceptual analysis of *X* is an attempt to provide a theory about what 'makes' something an *X*, by breaking the concept down into its more fundamental categories."[73] In relation to legal theory, the method investigates whether the expression 'law' can be reduced to more fundamental terms. Hart undertook this project by reducing law to primary and secondary rules, Raz by reducing law to authority.

The concept, created as such, must also "survive the method of possible cases,"[74] that is, present an account of the term which coheres with our intuitions. The "possible worlds," or "possible cases," approach, described in more detail below, relies on intuitions for determining the concept's scope. This is the most important facet of conceptual analysis: because the methodology attempts to examine the use of our terms, recourse to intuition about their appropriate use is essential. It is the folk concept which is elucidated in the case of law. My point is that you won't ever to get to the bottom of a social concept without taking account of how that concept is perceived by its participants. Law, as a social practice, is meaningless from a totally external perspective. Jackson suggests that when we seek to understand a concept, we are addressing that issue *according to our ordinary conception* of it.[75] In this sense, we determine our "ordinary conception" by analysing our intuition about various cases. This in turn gives rise to *our* theory, and "[t]o the extent that our intuitions coincide with the folk, they reveal the folk theory."[76] The factual content of the subject may, according to this picture, be mind-independent, but due to the variation in terms among people, the only way to explicate the content of that factual material is to systematically analyse those terms against our intuitions.

I will begin this discussion by exploring the famous attack launched by Quine on the project of conceptual analysis generally, before investigating the fallible nature of intuitions in philosophy specifically.

B. Quine's Critique of Conceptual Analysis

In one of his most famous publications, *Two Dogmas of Empiricism*,[77] Quine rejects the analytic-synthetic distinction, as introduced by Kant over 150 years

72 FRANK JACKSON, FROM METAPHYSICS TO ETHICS: A DEFENCE OF CONCEPTUAL ANALYSIS 28 (2000).
73 IAN P. FARRELL, *H.L.A. Hart and the Methodology of Jurisprudence* 84 TEX. L. REV. 983, 998 (2006).
74 JACKSON, *supra*, at 19.
75 *Id.* at 31.
76 *Id.* at 32.
77 WILLARD VAN ORMAN QUINE, TWO DOGMAS OF EMPIRICISM 60 PHIL. REV. 20 (1951).

previously.[78] The analytic-synthetic distinction is central to conceptual analysis. An analytic statement is one which is considered true solely by virtue of its meaning, such as, "all bachelors are unmarried." It is definitionally true. For Quine, we can only acquire knowledge of the world through experience of it, rather than relying on armchair philosophy: we cannot *know* that all bachelors are unmarried without direct experience of this phenomenon. Therefore, pre-Quine, it was widely acceptable in analytic philosophy to speak of truth by virtue of meaning alone. However, Quine argues that truth by definition alone is inadequate as part of the philosophical undertaking. in fact nothing definitive can be said about particular propositions in themselves; moreover, our belief system as an *entirety* (as well as its constituent elements) is subject to the "tribunal of experience" and any particular statement can be coerced into truth so long as sufficient changes are made to the belief system as a whole.[79] In short, there is no necessary distinction between conceptual truth and contingent truth. This is Quine's famous argument regarding confirmation holism. In other words, if evidence is brought to light which would appear to contradict a proposition, that evidence is not fatal to the proposition's status: instead, the statement can remain true so long as alterations are made elsewhere within the system of belief.[80] Therefore, both analytic and synthetic claims are revisable in light of conflicting evidence. As a logical corollary, then, analytic statements do not individually avoid the tribunal of experience, and thus cannot be deemed to be *necessarily* true.

For Quine, empirically confirming or infirming a statement defines its meaning. Therefore, the statement that "all bachelors are unmarried" cannot have meaning – such an investigation would simply result in circular argumentation, which is clearly undesirable. Knowledge of the world can only be *a posteriori*, *contra* Kant, and therefore concepts have no meaning in and of themselves, and can shed no light on the material world. I will now turn to the importance of the rejection of the analytic-synthetic distinction for conceptual analysis post-Quine.

C. Conceptual Analysis after Quine

Jackson is entirely conscious of the Quinean criticism in this regard. He therefore distinguishes between modest and immodest conceptual analysis. The immodest version draws conclusions based on conceptual intuitions

---

[78] *See* IMMANUEL KANT, CRITIQUE OF PURE REASON (1998). At 6-7, Kant notes:

> In all judgments in which the relation of a subject to the predicate is thought…this relation is possible in two different ways. Either the predicate *B* belongs to the subject *A* as something that is (covertly) contained in this concept *A*; or *B* lies entirely outside the concept *A*, though to be sure it stands in connection with it. In the first case, I call the judgment analytic, in the second synthetic.

[79] WILLARD VAN ORMAN QUINE, *Two Dogmas of Empiricism*, 60 PHIL. REV. 20, 38 (1951).

[80] *See, supra,* note 70.

(both individual and collective) about the intrinsic nature of the material world. This is dangerous, according to Jackson, because it "gives intuitions about possibilities too big a place in determining what the world is like."[81] A conceptual project of this type would accord intuitions a central status: if folk intuitions indicated that plants did not require sunlight for growth, this would form an important part of the concept of plant life. This type of analysis leaves no room for critical interaction with folk intuitions.

The more modest version does not accord intuitions such a status. This version "is not being given a role in determining the fundamental nature of our world; it is, rather, being given a central role in determining what to say in less fundamental terms given an account of the world stated in more fundamental terms."[82] Therefore, the analysis merely describes our concept of the world, not the world in itself. Jackson claims that this modest approach agrees in practice, "while dissenting in theory" from the Quinean critique.[83] This is so because the modest version does not purport to describe the material world in a representative manner, and thus does not rely on empirical evidence for its validity. All that it claims to do is to describe our *concept* of the world: the way we interpret the world, regardless of what lies without.

Jackson appears to adhere to the 'Kripke counter-approach' to conceptual analysis, which is an attempt at saving conceptual analysis from the threat of Quine. In response to Quine, Jackson notes that "[t]he possible worlds approach is one way of responding to this challenge."[84] In this context, Kripke has attempted to rescue analytic philosophy by constructing an idea of necessity that is not based on conceptual truth.[85] He substitutes an account of conceptual meaning with an account of metaphysical meaning with his idea of "possible worlds." Kripke has thereby constructed the notion that there are many possible worlds, and the necessity of meaning is tested against these worlds. Under the process of rigid designation, a naming event occurs where we attach a name to an entity. Once we have attached the name, anything we later find out about the substance is necessarily true, because it is true in every possible world where the naming event took place. Fodor exemplifies this well:

> [T]here are worlds that are just like ours except that there's nobody in them, and worlds just like ours except that everybody is in them except President Bush…Notice, however, that there is no (possible) world in which 2+2=5; and none in which bachelors are

---

81 JACKSON, *supra*, at 43-44.
82 *Id.* at 44.
83 *Id.*
84 *Id.* at 46.
85 SAUL KRIPKE, NAMING AND NECESSITY (1980).

> married...Here we seem to have a non-conceptual notion of necessity.[86]

However, if conceptual analysis is gone, reliance on intuition remains. Fodor refers to Hilary Putnam's twin-earth dilemma in this regard. If one were to discover a substance which was identical to water in every way but was made of a different substance, (for example, made of XYZ rather than H_20) would our intuitions guide us in concluding that it is water? According to Putnam, our intuition would say that it is not water, and that it is necessarily and *a priori* not water, because it is not water in *every possible world.* Even if all of our intuitions were in agreement on this matter, Fodor questions whether intuitions can yield truth at all: "some story is needed about what makes such intuitions true (or false) about what possible worlds there are and, as far as I can see, the only candidates are facts about concepts."[87] Therefore, Quine's criticisms still stand.

Jackson offers his modest approach as a nod to Quine, and while he endorses the Kripkean response as a method of providing *a priori* truths for conceptual analysis, these *a priori* truths will only be true of the concept, not of the world itself.[88] Nevertheless, I will not here concern myself with the extent to which Quine undermines Jackson's project, or indeed, the extent to which Kripke undermines Quine's project. Instead, what is here argued is that an appeal to intuitions in analytic philosophy remains unavoidable and it is this appeal which renders analyticity fallible. In this context, Bix pointedly asks: "[i]s conceptual analysis of law, in the end, merely a quasi-sociological investigation into one's community's linguistic intuitions?"[89] The answer to this appears to be a resounding yes. I will argue in Part V that an appeal to intuitions renders the jurisprudential endeavour fallible, and therefore undermines any claims which it makes to essentiality in explicating the nature of law.

V. INTUITIONS IN PHILOSOPHY

Sosa points to the fact that "[p]hilosophy has perennially relied on what seems intuitively right to the reflective mind."[90] An intuition is a judgment which is not made on the basis of some kind of explicit reasoning process which a person can consciously observe. Intuitions are fundamentally important in the analysis of social concepts, and are thus central to the hermeneutic method.

---

[86] JERRY FODOR, *Water's Water Everywhere*, 26 LONDON REV. BOOKS Oct. 21, 2004, at 18.

[87] *Id.* at 18.

[88] JACKSON, *supra*, at 49.

[89] BRIAN BIX, *Joseph Raz and Conceptual Analysis* 60-65 UNI. MINN. LAW SCHOOL LEGAL STUDIES RESEARCH PAPER SERIES 11.

[90] ERNEST SOSA, *Intuitions and Truth*, *in* P. Greenough & M.P. Lynch ed., TRUTH AND REALISM 208 (2006).

As noted above, hermeneutic concepts differ from natural kind concepts in that they influence the way in which we understand ourselves, and in the way that the hermeneutic function fixes the concept's extension.[91] A theory of law must therefore account for the intuitions of those partaking in a social practice if it is to be a successful social theory. I will examine the role of intuition in conceptual analysis, and will proceed to analyse the methodology of intuition in the contexts of reflective equilibrium and cognitive diversity.

A. Intuitions and Folk Theory

It is generally accepted that insofar as a theorist's intuition coincide with the intuitions of the folk within a social practice, the folk theory of that concept is revealed. For Jackson, this means that the "general coincidence in intuitive responses to the Gettier examples reveals something about the folk theory of knowledge in the sense of revealing what governs folk ascriptions of knowledge."[92] The Gettier counter-examples are a series of problems which question the traditional definition of knowledge as justified true belief.[93] One of the counter-examples reads thus: Smith is justified in believing the false proposition that (i) Jones owns a Ford. On the basis of (i), Smith infers, and is thus justified in believing, that (ii) either Jones owns a Ford or that Brown is in Barcelona. As it happens, Brown is in Barcelona, and so (ii) is true. Therefore, although Smith is justified in believing (ii), he does not *know* (ii). These are cases where a person has a justified true belief that *x* but does not know *x*. There has been overwhelming agreement as to the results given in the counter-examples and thus they were initially seen to offer a new insight into the folk theory by virtue of general intuition. However, it will be seen from the discussion below that the Gettier counter-examples do nothing more than testify to the fact that intuitions about knowledge differ from person to person, and from region to region, a fact which is detrimental to the methodology of reliance on intuitions in arriving at folk theory.

Jackson argues that in order to reveal the folk theory, all one has to do is extend, or project one's own intuition about possible cases onto the intuitions of others: "often we know that our own case is typical and so can generalize from it to others."[94] That is, we can generalize our own intuitions to that of the folk since we share the same folk theory. However, faithfulness to the intuitions of the folk is subject to two provisos. First, Jackson argues that if our audience happens to be theoretical physicists, and the subject is phrased in

[91] FARRELL, *supra*, at 1002. Natural kind concepts are those concepts whose extension is fixed by whatever scientific generalizations employ the concept. Further, their boundaries will not be defined by the attitudes people have towards them.
[92] JACKSON, *supra*, at 32.
[93] EDMUND GETTIER, *Is Justified True Belief Knowledge?* 23 ANALYSIS 112 (1963).
[94] JACKSON, *supra*, at 37.

terms of theoretical physics, "it would be the intuitions and stipulations of this special subset of the folk that would hold centre stage."[95] Second, we should be prepared to make sensible adjustments to folk concepts where this is required. A limited massaging of the intuitions of the folk is thus acceptable. This can be done, according to Jackson, due to the objective nature of folk theory:

> I take it that it is part of current folk morality that convergence will or would occur. We have some kind of commitment to the idea that moral disagreements can be resolved by sufficient critical reflection – which is why we bother to engage in moral debate. To that extent, some sort of objectivism is part of current folk morality.[96]

This statement is indicative of the reflective nature of Jackson's conceptual analysis. The objectivism mentioned is in fact simply the result of conscious reflection about possible cases via theoretical reflection. Therefore, it becomes necessary to examine whether objectivism can in fact be achieved through cognitive reflection, and if it cannot, whether presumptions to this effect are detrimental to the conceptual methodology.

B. The Importance of Intuitions for Reflective Equilibrium

Reflective equilibrium is a method of engaging in controlled thought-experiments, initiated by Goodman and made popular in more recent times by Rawls.[97] Because concepts are entities which are not immediately available to us, engaged reflection is seen to be necessary for their explication. The method of reflective equilibrium is "widely used to characterize a system of principles and judgments that have been brought into coherence with one another…"[98] Therefore, a set of observations about the concept is made, and a theory is constructed to account for those observations. Where there is recalcitrant data, it may be dismissed as faulty or irrelevant. However, where recalcitrant data is impossible to dismiss, the theory will have to be altered. Revisions are thus subjectively carried out, according to the intuitions of the theorist. The theory is tested against intuitions about cases which are imagined, and the resultant intuition about that case will then play a firm role in theory construction. The theory will subsequently be used to make predictions about cases on which intuition has not been consulted, "or on cases that were not part of the intuitive base from which the theory was

95 *Id.* at 46-47.

96 *Id.* at 137.

97 *See generally*, JOHN RAWLS, *A Theory of Justice* (2nd ed., Harvard University Press, 1971); NELSON GOODMAN, *Fact, Fiction and Forecast* (Harvard University Press, 1955).

98 STEPHEN STICH, *Reflective Equilibrium, Analytic Epistemology and the Problem of Cognitive Diversity*, *in* DePaul & Ramsey eds., RETHINKING INTUITION: THE PSYCHOLOGY OF INTUITION AND ITS ROLE IN PHILOSOPHICAL INQUIRY 97 (1998).

generated."[99] Intuitions therefore have a central role to play in the analysis. Cummins thus notes:

> If we want to criticize reflective equilibrium, then, we are squarely reduced to asking what authority the intuitions themselves have; to asking, that is, whether intuition can play the role observation plays in science.[100]

Cummins argues that in science, conflicting propositions must be explained away in some objective fashion, in order to maintain its credibility as a discipline. For example, if there is a disagreement as to whether the night sky rotates clockwise or anti-clockwise, there would have to be a method for resolving the dispute; agreeing to disagree would simply not be satisfactory under the circumstances. On the other hand, reflective theory cannot resolve disputes that arise about the evidence in question, in the main because it is common for theorists to presume that there is intuitive agreement, and this gives rise to a selection effect, substantially weakening the theory. Cummins concludes that the methodology is epistemologically useless, untrustworthy, inaccurate and biased.

There are degrees of reflective equilibrium employed by philosophers of the social sciences. Although many philosophers will not explicitly adhere to the method, testing intuitions and bringing results of such tests into coherence is a common feature of current analytic philosophy. Hintikka argues that true reflective equilibrium is in fact difficult to come by: "the vast majority of appeals to intuitions by contemporary philosophers cannot be conceived as controlled thought experiments nor be justified by recasting them as such."[101] Regardless of degree, however, the method is a flawed one. In attempting to achieve intuitive consensus, the theorist moves uneasily between the consensus of the populous in ideal deliberative conditions and *de facto* consensus. Stich is critical of this approach, noting that "one influential proposal for solving the problem of cognitive diversity, a proposal that invokes the notion of reflective equilibrium, will not work."[102] Reflective equilibrium is an inherently subjective method of analysis and therefore cannot give rise to general and necessary truths about the nature of a social practice. Even if an assumption of cognitive uniformity is true, the theory does not itself harbor truth: once new evidence comes to light the theory must be redrawn to accord with the empirical data and therefore nothing essential can be revealed as a result of the process.

---

99 ROBERT CUMMINS, *Reflection on Reflective Equilibrium*, *in* DePaul & Ramsey eds., RETHINKING INTUITION, *supra*, at 114.

100 *Id.* at 115.

101 JAAKKO HINTIKKA, *The Emporer's New Intuitions* 96 J. PHIL. 127, 147 (1999).

102 STICH, *supra*, at 95.

I will now proceed to the hotly contested notion of cognitive diversity.

C. Cognitive Diversity

It is argued here that presumptions of cognitive uniformity are generally hasty and blind. Cognitive diversity is a very real phenomenon in society and is an issue which is significantly overlooked in current jurisprudential thought. Folk theory, as employed by conceptual analysts, is not a grand narrative of attitudes in society and ultimately must be differentiated to accommodate for distinctions in societal attitudes.

Weinberg, Stich and Nichols have made important developments in this regard.[103] Their research indicates that the Gettier counter-examples report nothing more than specific facts about the intuitions of subgroups in society. The research reveals that different people in different socio-economic classes and ethnic groups have systematically different intuitions about particular cases.

In a thought-experiment, Weinberg et al. found that intuitions in fact do not maintain uniformity from culture to culture. One problem posed during their research read thus:

> Bob has a friend, Jill, who has driven a Buick for many years. Bob therefore thinks that Jill drives an American car. He is not aware, however, that her Buick has recently been stolen, and he is also not aware that Jill has replaced it with a Pontiac, which is a different kind of American car. Does Bob really know that Jill drives an American car, or does he only believe it?[104]

75% of subjects with a European background answered that Bob "only believes," with 25% stating that Bob "really knows." However, interestingly, members of other cultural backgrounds had dramatically different intuitions. 57% of people whose cultural background was East Asian and 61% of subjects whose cultural background was Indian or Pakistani answered that Bob "really knows."[105]

Stich also refers to the work of Richard Nisbett, who has "shown that there are large and systematic differences between East Asians and Westerners on a long list of cognitive processes including perception, attention and memory."

---

[103] Leiter refers to this research in his discussion of naturalism. *See* LEITER, *supra*, at 47.

[104] JONATHAN M. WEINBERG, et al., *Normativity and Epistemic Intuitions* 29 PHIL. TOPICS 429, 441-448 (2001).

[105] *Id.*

Furthermore, Stich refers to a series of cases, including those presented by Jonathan Haidt et al., in which significantly different moral intuitions arose as between different socio-economic classes in society.[106]

On a similar note, Wisniewski argues that studies proving what seem like legitimate intuitive responses to draw are actually found to be wrong in many cases. He thus warns: "[i]t is clear that researchers must be very careful about relying on their own intuitions in formulating theories of thought and behaviour. Experimental methods are absolutely essential for determining the validity of such intuitions."[107]

Gopnik and Schwitzgebel have also done important work in this area. They argue that 20th century physics, for example, has "notoriously shown the inaccuracy of our everyday intuitions about the nature of space and time…"[108] For them, lay intuitions are often used as a foundation for a theory, which is then applied to other domains by analogy and they argue that philosophers who do this, "have notoriously violated the intuitions of folk psychology."[109]

Although it will often be possible to predict the intuitions of others when their mentalities are well known to us, this will not always be successful, particularly where the subjects of the analysis originate from different ethnic or socio-economic backgrounds. Habermas, in outlining his theory of deliberative democracy, gives the example of parents of children from different cultural groups not arriving at parent-teaching meetings. While it might be tempting to conclude that they are simply not interested in taking part in the meeting, it is possible that an examination of their *own* intuitions would reveal very different motivations for not arriving, such as an unwillingness to be judged by members of the foreign culture, or financial constraints in obtaining transport. For Habermas, this is a warning against the superimposition of preconceptions from the theorist to her subjects. On a practical level, where that superimposition occurs, the voices of philosophical subjects would be lost on the theorist and thus communication at this most basic level can alter the development of the theory tremendously.

In sum, folk intuitions cannot be said to be universal, even where they are employed for the modest purpose of describing our concept alone. Leiter argues that there is little reason to believe that such cognitive diversity would not also apply to the concept of law. Indeed, he notes that the Oxfordian

---

106 WEINBERG et al., *supra*, at Section 3.

107 EDWARD J. WISNIEWSKI, *The Psychology of Intuition*, *in* DePaul and Ramsey eds., RETHINKING INTUITION, *supra*.

108 ALISON GOPNIK & ERIC SCHWITZGEBEL, *Whose Concepts are They, Anyway? The Role of Philosophical Intuition in Empirical Psychology*, *in* DePaul & Ramsey eds., *supra*, at 78.

109 *Id*, at 83.

jurisprudential world has dominated the scene for over 50 years and that this is likely to have a selection effect on the relevant weight accorded to different intuitions in analysing law.[110]

If intuitions are ethnically and socio-economically situated, therefore, it is unsatisfactory for the theorist to arbitrarily impose her own intuitions onto the intuitions of members of society, as is the case in analytic legal philosophy in general. Ultimately, this process will not demonstrate the truth of the folk theory. As noted above, intuitions are an essential part of (i) delineating what is significant and important about features of the legal system, and (ii) demonstrating the truth of a given theory of a concept of law. During the process of theory construction, the philosopher's apparent reference to folk intuitions in delineating her subject matter, and the same reference in testing the success of her theory, can be nothing more than a blind guess, based on highly subjective considerations. The theorist can thus either carry out opinion polls to discover the intuitions of those within its subject matter,[111] and assert the truth of the resultant theory as geographically and temporally limited, or the theorist can do what she has always done – remain in her armchair – and accept the very fallible nature of her results.

D. Conceptual Analysis, Intuitions and Positivism

I will now examine the fate of legal positivism in light of the foregoing discussion.[112] A majority of analytic legal positivists seeks to provide an account of law which explicates its *essential* features: features which arise necessarily in every legal system. Austin notes that analytic jurisprudence strives for "the essence or nature which is common to all laws that are properly so called."[113] I will examine the positivist school in relation to the theories of Hart and Raz in particular.

Let us recap on Hart's self-proclaimed goal in legal theory:

> My aim in this book was to provide a theory of law which is both general and descriptive. It is *general* in the sense that it is not tied to any particular legal system or legal culture, but seeks to give an explanatory and clarifying account of law…My account is *descriptive* in that it is morally neutral and has no justificatory aims…[114]

---

[110] LEITER, *supra*, at 48-49.

[111] This would more properly become a sociological inquiry rather than an analytic one.

[112] While my focus will be on positivism in this regard, the following discussion is relevant for all legal philosophy which relies on conceptual analysis and intuitions as part of its philosophical armoury.

[113] AUSTIN, *supra*, at 11.

[114] HART, CONCEPT OF LAW, *supra*, at 239-240. Emphasis original.

The second tenet of this claim, namely, the possibility of description for legal theory, has been examined in Part III. What is relevant for my present purpose is to explore the possibility of *general* jurisprudence.

Hart seeks to describe the institution of law in a universal fashion. He is undoubtedly engaging in conceptual analysis in his undertaking, whether of a modest or an immodest nature.[115] He is seeking to explicate the *concept* of law, something which he considers to give rise to universal truths about the nature of law. My goal here is to point out that positivism cannot yield general truths by virtue of its use of conceptual analysis and its consequent use of intuition-pumping. This will be demonstrated below.

Raz is also concerned with general jurisprudence: he notes that a theory of law is "a set of systematically related *true* propositions about the nature of law."[116] Raz's primary objective is to provide an account of law which highlights its *essential* features, those features which differentiate it from other social institutions. "At its most fundamental, legal philosophy is an inquiry into the nature of law, and the fundamental features of legal institutions and practices."[117] He is of the view that legal theory has universal application, "that it – when successful – provides an account of the nature of law, wherever and whenever it is to be found."[118] However, Raz is quick to differentiate between the *concept* of an entity and its *nature*: concepts are a "philosophical creation"[119] and constitute "how we conceive aspects of the world, and lie between words and their meaning, in which they are expressed, on the one side, and the nature of things to which they apply on the other."[120] For Raz, legal theories are theories of the concept of law.[121] Nevertheless, "[a]n explanation of a

---

115 A number of commentators have emphasized the modest nature of Hart's conceptual analysis. *Eg.* VERONICA RODERIGUEZ-BLANCO, *A Defence of Hart's Semantics as Nonambitious Conceptual Analysis, supra*; *See also* FARRELL, *supra*, at 998. On the other hand, Coleman implies that Hart's is a form of immodest conceptual analysis. *See generally* COLEMAN, METHODOLOGY, *supra*.

116 JOSEPH RAZ, *Can There Be a Theory of Law*, *in* Martin P. Golding & William A. Edmundson eds., THE BLACKWELL GUIDE TO THE PHILOSOPHY OF LAW AND LEGAL THEORY 324 (2005). Emphasis added.

117 RAZ, TWO VIEWS, *supra*, at 3.

118 RAZ, *Can There Be a Theory of Law*, *supra*, at 340. For a critique of this article, *see* ROBERT ALEXY, *On Two Juxtapositions: Concept and Nature, Law and Philosophy: Some Comments on Joseph Raz's "Can There Be a Theory of Law"* 20 RATIO JURIS 162 (2007). Alexy agrees with the possibility of the universality of the nature of law but takes issue with Raz's description of the concept as exclusively parochial and with his contention that legal philosophy cannot be part of the law.

119 RAZ, *Can There Be a Theory of Law*, *supra*, at 324.

120 *Id.* at 325.

121 Raz also describes adjudication by virtue of the *concept* of adjudication rather than explicating its nature. He notes that his observations "are meant to be faithful to the accepted theory of the practice rather than to the practice itself." *See* JOSEPH RAZ, THE AUTHORITY OF LAW, *supra*, at 181.

concept involves explaining the feature through which it applies to its object or property, but also explaining more broadly the *nature* of the object or property that it is a concept of."[122] Concepts may be similar, but not identical to, law's nature, and it is an analysis of the latter which is the main task of jurisprudence. For Raz, any successful theory of law both explains the law and contains propositions that are *necessarily* true about it. Thus, "the essential properties of the law are universal characteristics of law."[123] According to Raz, the fact that law has an essential nature does not imply that it cannot change over time, it simply means that when what was once law has sufficiently changed, it will enter a transition and will no longer be law thereafter. Our concepts are thus parochial and subject to change, whereas the nature of law is universal. However, where there are different concepts of law in existence at any given time, it is *our* concept which is fundamental: "it is our concept of law which calls the shots: other concepts are concepts of law if and only if they are related in appropriate ways to our concepts."[124] Therefore, according to Raz, there can be societies which do not share our concept of law but who still 'have' law. However, the lurking question throughout Raz's discussion is this: if the nature of law and the concept of law can be differentiated, one yielding universal truths and the other offering parochial narratives, how is that we are to explicate the *nature* of law? If Raz's central claim is to insist on the possibility of universal and objective legal foundations, how does he suppose we go about this task? He ends on a modest note:

That does not establish that a theory of law is in principle possible, or that if it is possible it can achieve objective knowledge…To positively establish the possibility of a theory of law we need to examine the nature of explanation and of objectivity.[125]

Therefore, objectivity does not arise out of an analysis based on concepts. Although Raz purports to be discovering the nature of law through the use of conceptual analysis, he cannot sustain the position that anything mind-independent or objective is in fact revealed through this methodology. Stavropoulos explains objectivity well:

> In a classic approach, a domain is objective in case the existence and character of the objects that populate the domain is independent of the mind, that is, of thoughts, beliefs, desires, and other aspects of the mental. This approach puts the emphasis on the world, and treats the standing of our thoughts or beliefs about these objects as derivative. It says that our thoughts or beliefs about these objects are capable of

122 RAZ, TWO VIEWS, *supra*, at 8. Emphasis added.
123 RAZ, *Can There Be a Theory of Law*, *supra*, at 328.
124 *Id.* at 332.
125 *Id.* at 340.

> being objective in virtue of the fact that reality contains the objects that it does…[126]

Of course, mind-independence is notoriously difficult to define. I will assume for our sake that objective truths hold independently of our thoughts and beliefs. Therefore, there is a logical space, to use Stavropoulos' terms, between how we understand things and how they actually are. The goal of positivism is to uncover aspects of the law which are mind-independent and therefore not limited temporally or geographically. Even if the law has some universal nature, I argue that this essential core cannot be explicated by employing conceptual analysis. Unlike science, there is no standard of reference by which the social practice of law can be measured. Statements about concepts cannot be verified or falsified directly, unlike statements about the objects of natural sciences. There may be certain practices within the legal system which can be enumerated, but the question: "what is the concept of law" will never produce answers that reveal law's nature if conceptual analysis is at the heart of the theorist's methodology. If beliefs regarding law are 'false,' there is no way for the theorist to correct them, except to use her own system of beliefs as a standard, which cannot give rise to objective results.

Nevertheless, positivism seeks to lay bare truths about the *nature* of law based on its elucidation of the concept of law. There is no doubt that Hart seeks to explicate the *concept* of law; his primary work goes by that very name. On the other hand, while Raz is aware of the limits of conceptual analysis, he does not avoid the charge of limiting himself to results which are local. His account of authority is an account of the *concept* of authority; his account of law is an account of the *concept* of law. He does not adequately explain how an analysis of the concept of law can lead us to an understanding of the nature of law. Thus it is my claim that concepts cannot take us any closer to an entity's nature: if anything, they will only distort its nature. On the one hand Raz is a fierce advocate of essentialism,[127] on the other, he accepts the fact that a methodology for discovering the objective nature of law yet has to be developed.[128] In the meantime, he remains satisfied to employ conceptual analysis. This, admittedly, is modest conceptual analysis but it does not exempt him from error since, as noted above, even modest conceptual analysis cannot offer truths which are essential in character.

Conceptual analysis, as employed by both Hart and Raz, clearly requires a dependence on the intuitions of legal subjects. The limited nature of its results must thus be accepted. Hart relies on the convergence of the use of language

126 NICOS STAVROPOULOS, *Objectivity*, *in* Martin P. Golding & William A. Edmundson eds., THE BLACKWELL GUIDE, *supra*, at 315.

127 *See*, *supra*, note 114.

128 *See*, *supra*, note 116.

of his subjects, but this assumes the fact that there *is* convergence. The discussion of the Gettier counter-examples above highlights the fact that not all people at all in times in all places will agree on linguistic definitions. Particularly when it comes to legal practice, there is no precise definition of many terms and even if there is general consensus, there will always be peripheral dissenters – which then requires the theorist to prioritise the majority of linguistic users according to his intuition of which category of users is correct. This assumption is nothing more than a superimposition of Hart's intuitions onto those who are the subject of his inquiry. Raz's description of authority falls into the same error.

There may be characteristics which are essential to law, in the sense that law must harbor them in order for it to be law, but any investigation into this essential nature based on concepts requires a subjective analysis which is limited to the attitudes of a subset of the participants within the legal system. In addition to this, even a modest claim to be describing the *concept* of law alone, and not its universal nature, is a fallible enterprise based on the preceding discussion about intuitions.

Williamson cogently argues that we "should face the fact that evidence is always liable to be contested in philosophy, and stop using talk of intuition to disguise this unpleasant fact from ourselves."[129] He correctly points out the anomaly that positivism prides itself on its rigor, and yet remains satisfied to rely on a methodology which has no epistemic foundation whatsoever. Obviously all methodologies fall into this very trap – but the point is that positivism (unlike many schools of jurisprudence) continues to reject this criticism in going about its task – and I think it's very important that positivists begin to take heed of it instead of ploughing on in denial. Based on the foregoing, there is little to say that the positivist's findings are anything more than an account of the theorist's subjective reflections, verified by an uncertain number of subjects within the legal community. Therefore, if positivism's claim to essentiality does not hold, it is important to examine how the future of the jurisprudential endeavor is to proceed.

VI. THE FUTURE OF LEGAL THEORY

Can armchair jurisprudence be abandoned on the basis that it does not yield necessary truth? The response to this proposal has been diverse. I will begin by examining three prominent positions which have been advanced as alternatives to traditional analytic positivism in this regard.

A. A Postmodernist Approach

[129] TIMOTHY WILLIAMSON, *Philosophical 'Intuitions' and Scepticism about Judgement* 58 DIALECTICA 109, 109 (2004).

The postmodernist school of thought is acutely aware of the problem of essentiality, or lack thereof, facing legal theory today. Despite its inherent ability to evade definition, it is generally agreed that postmodernism is skeptical of the analytic agenda of achieving grand theory in the form of structured, inter-subjective truths. The postmodernist approach to theory has been introduced into jurisprudence most prominently by Balkin.

Balkin argues that reality is changed through interpretation. While there may be mind-independent entities, such entities are not comprehensible or explicable in their independent form. Therefore, universal characteristics are not discoverable through any of our current philosophical mechanisms. As a result, Balkin vehemently opposes the possibility of grand theory in jurisprudence. Instead of constantly striving for it, he suggests an alternative: an approach embracing cognitive diversity by exploring the subject in all its forms. He therefore proposes, "to understand the nature of law we must understand the nature of legal understanding."[130]

According to Balkin, as we interpret entities, the subject's horizons fuse with those of the entity, and, once interpreted, both the subject and the entity are respectively changed. When examining something like the nature of coherence in law, therefore, it is important that the theorist focuses on the legal subject *as well as* the legal object. Legal concepts such as coherence are not, according to Balkin, pre-existent but instead are the result of judgments made by the legal subject when reflecting on law. Therefore, legal theorists should develop a "jurisprudence of the subject;"[131] one which recognizes that questions about the nature of law must be concerned "with the ideological, sociological and psychological features of our understanding of the legal system."[132] He notes that:

> These cultural norms and frameworks of understanding are not simply superimposed on an individual's preexisting beliefs; they constitute her and form part of what makes her an individual. Subjectivity is what the individual subject brings to the act of understanding; it is what allows her to construct the object of her interpretation so that she can understand it.[133]

---

130 JACK M. BALKIN, *Understanding Legal Understanding* 105 YALE L. J. 103, 106 (1993-1994). Balkin seems to use "nature" here to refer to legal *characteristics* rather than the *essential* properties of law.

131 *Id.* at 107.

132 *Id.*

133 *Id.*

Balkin's objective in this regard is to view the subject[134] and object[135] of legal interpretation as equal partners in the construction of the legal system. For him, subjectivity is not necessarily individuality, since shared ideologies can give rise to shared outward understanding. He likens ideology to "cultural software,"[136] a copy of which is given to each of us, so that where our copies are similar, we will experience a type of shared understanding. Embedded cultural ideology means that "the beholder is not fully in control of what she sees."[137] She can only make judgments *through* her ideology and cannot choose the terms of her ideology or social construction.

Balkin's objection to theorizing which ignores the legal subject revolves around the issue of projection: the ideology of the theorist who ignores the legal subject is consequently superimposed onto that of the subject, not only making the subject's influence on the legal concept seem invisible, but also misdescribing the legal concept.

For Balkin, legal understanding is a purposive activity, and there are as many possible descriptions of law as there are purposes. Judgments of legal coherence arise out of one particular form of understanding, which Balkin terms *rational reconstruction.* This is the attempt to see reason in legal materials, to see them as a plausible and sensible means of human regulation. Such judgments rest upon our psychological needs: our need to make sense of the world and to preserve our belief in our own coherence.

However, rational reconstruction is only one form of understanding, and Balkin duly points out that there are many internal participants, as well as many different purposes attributed to law by each relevant subgroup. The biggest problem with analytic theorists, then, is their tendency to categorize according to one or other subgroup, and to brand this subjective subdivision as a general and objective theory of law:

By forgetting the different purposes of understanding and the socially situated nature of understanding, they may elevate a particular form of understanding, useful as it may be in a particular context and for a particular purpose, to a universal status.[138]

Despite Balkin's reluctance to generalize the diverse nature of internal perspectives and purposes of actors in law, he nevertheless adopts a critical

134 In this context, consistent with Balkin's use of the terms, "subject" refers to the interpreter and "object" refers to the object of study.

135 *Id.*

136 *Id.* at 108.

137 *Id.*

138 *Id.* at 136.

perspective towards the attitudes of the participants in the legal system.[139] In the end, the theorist's own ideology will always be imposed onto the subject with this type of critical approach, and Balkin thus finds himself in the same position which he wishes to escape, thereby avoiding the problem of cognitive diversity rather than solving it. Intuition is an important feature of Balkin's approach: he is an armchair theorist after all. Intuition, while fallible, therefore appears to be utterly unavoidable, even for the postmodernist. Although postmodernism claims to be sceptical about any kind of blind assertions of truth,[140] Lynch correctly notes that "[w]hen engaging in inquiry, no matter how carefully, *something* is always being taken for granted as immediately obvious."[141] Even at our most sceptical, we cannot question everything at once. *Something* must remain fixed, and in the end, that something will be intuition. Williamson argues that "[a]t some point we are entitled to hold on to what we know, and apply it," even if what we 'know' is objectively fallible. For him, even though "[o]ur fallibility about our evidence is unavoidable; we have no alternative but to muddle through as best we can." A despondent conclusion, perhaps, but one which seeks to avoid the disadvantages of postmodernism, a method which appears to amount to an endless search for something that remains forever beyond our grasp.

This discussion highlights an important point of concern for all theorists: the extent to which we are willing to take certain facts for granted in order to begin from a stable philosophical foundation, and to thereby work our way up. If nothing is taken for granted, a postmodernist approach ensues, and infinite questioning is at large. Although this project is insightful on the basis that it does not create any elaborate fictions of truth or necessity, and instead embraces the impossibility of truth in all its forms, progress cannot be made with such an approach. Postmodernism may have no qualms about this, but many people do. In the end, it seems that a choice must be made between the search for universal and objective truth and the desire for progress in a pragmatic sense. Even if pomo is a more accurate depiction of the state of the universe, it hinders progress, and so a choice between accuracy/truth and pragmatics/progress must be made.

If the postmodernist method is honest on the one hand, it is counter-productive for theory building on the other. Even if we were accept that what pomo discovers is closer to truth than what other theorists discover, we care about formalizations, at least if we believe in the possibility of and desire to

139 Balkin argues thus: "I believe that we must ground jurisprudence in a critical perspective, one that employs ideological critique to reflect on our internal experience of law." *See* BALKIN, *supra*, at 110.

140 It should be noted that modernism also adopts this position.

141 MICHAEL P. LYNCH, *Trusting Intuitions*, *in* P. Greenough & M.P. Lynch eds., TRUTH AND REALISM, *supra*, at 236.

attain progress. If the objective of theory is to categorize reality in order that coherence may be developed through application by analogy, postmodernism cannot contribute to this goal. Of course, this is well understood by the postmodernist, who does not consider progress or pragmatism worthy aims, but rather, seeks only understanding of the world in its purest form. Nevertheless, for the many theorists who do value progress, postmodernism in its extreme form simply will not do.

An important obstacle which theorists such as Balkin face is that of infinite regression – if everything is socially constructed, there is no stopping place for evaluation and thus no end point for theory: theory becomes nothing more than a series of infinite ponderings. Again, infinite regression is a feature of theory which is embraced by the postmodernist, who does not consider finality a plausible objective. Postmodernism has highlighted the fallibility of general claims to truth, a conclusion which the author agrees with based on the foregoing discussion about theoretical reliance on intuitionism. However, if we wish to avoid the consequent infinite regress which the postmodernist movement encourages, we must ask ourselves which path our philosophical task must take. I argue here that law is a practice which is best described from a pragmatic point of view, a discussion I return to in Section D. In the meantime, I will examine a position which stands in stark contrast to postmodernism: naturalization.

B. Jurisprudence Naturalized

Quine's critique of analytic philosophy has prompted theorists to adopt a naturalistic approach to philosophy generally. Consequently, Brian Leiter has introduced naturalism into legal theory.

I will begin by reviewing Quine's naturalistic position. The problem with reconstructive science, according to Quine, is that the theory is built up from a series of observations which themselves depend on subjective input.[142] Leiter notes in this context:

> The naturalist, following Quine, rejects the idea that there could be a "first philosophy," a philosophical solution to problems that proceeds a priori, that is, prior to any experience. Instead, the philosophical naturalist demands continuity with the natural and social sciences…[143]

---

[142] WILLARD VAN ORMAN QUINE, *Epistemology Naturalized, in* W.V.O. QUINE, ONTOLOGICAL RELATIVITY AND OTHER ESSAYS (1969).I have touched on this issue above in Part III in the context of both Popper and Kuhn.

[143] BRIAN LEITER, *Rethinking Legal Realism: Towards a Naturalized Jurisprudence* 76(2) TEX. L. REV. 288, 289 (1997).

According to Quine, although psychology itself is not an entirely objective methodology, results which can be obtained by examining the output of environmental stimuli will find uniformity in a shared external world. The naturalization of epistemology is concerned with relating controlled input of information to the subsequent output, thereby understanding more profoundly the relationship between material evidence and the theory developed as a result of that evidence. For Quine, therefore, it is "[b]etter to discover how science is in fact developed and learned than to fabricate a fictitious structure to a similar effect."[144]

Based on the failure of concepts and intuitions in philosophy, Leiter also takes refuge in naturalized jurisprudence as the only methodology which he considers reliable. Leiter argues that the science of human cognition ought to replace armchair psychology. Epistemology should be naturalized as a more progressive way of theorizing about the world. Neither moral nor epistemic norms are foundational, and cannot be explicated from the armchair. Rather, "normative theorizing must be continuous with scientific theorizing."[145] It is an *a posteriori* matter as to which norms in fact serve our epistemic or cognitive goals. Leiter argues:

> [T]he only sound reason to prefer one metaphysical or epistemological picture over another is not because it seems intuitively obvious...but because it earns its place by facilitating successful *a posteriori* theories of the world....Philosophy, on this naturalistic story, has no special methods for investigating the world; it is simply the abstract and reflective part of empirical science.[146]

Therefore, theories of law should only be verifiable empirically: all attempts at analytic jurisprudence should be abandoned, or at the very least, relegated to a subset of the natural sciences. There is no first philosophy; instead, philosophy is the abstract branch of empiricism.

Leiter argues that naturalization itself may not be empirically verifiable as a method of analysis. He refers to Neurath's boat in this regard: we cannot climb out of the structure and rebuild it from without. Instead, we must choose which planks to rest upon while reconstructing the boat on pragmatic grounds. The theory, according to Leiter, is not superior for *a priori* reasons,

---

144 W.V.O. QUINE, *Epistemology Naturalized*, *supra*, at 78.

145 BRIAN LEITER, *Naturalism and Naturalized Jurisprudence*, *in* Brian Bix eds., ANALYSING LAW: NEW ESSAYS IN LEGAL THEORY 90 (1998).

146 LEITER, *Beyond the Hart/Dworkin Debate*, *supra*, at 50. *See also* LEITER, *Rethinking Legal Realism: Toward a Naturalized Jurisprudence* 76 TEX. L. REV. 267 (1997); LEITER, NATURALIZING JURISPRUDENCE: ESSAYS ON AMERICAN LEGAL REALISM AND NATURALISM IN LEGAL PHILOSOPHY (2007).

but rather, because it has "delivered the goods." In short, it has proved successful in predicting the nature of the external world. He notes that "it sends planes into the sky, eradicates certain cancerous growths, makes possible the storage of millions of pages of data on a tiny chip, and the like."[147]

The argument for naturalism is an interesting attempt to avoid the limitations presented by conceptual analysis, but is ultimately a questionable approach in the context of law. Quine's philosophy refers to the shared external understanding of concepts that exist within the observable world. Disagreements about law are never verifiable or falsifiable on empirical grounds because law is a social construct which can only comprehensibly be described via the perceptions of the participants – which means that there is no empirical yardstick for measuring the accuracy or otherwise of each perspective on the law. Thus, we may never actually reach consensus about the nature of law, and thus naturalism does not appear to apply in the same way. Indeed, Bix argues against Leiter that empirical observation is unlikely to settle contests between theorists as to the correct way of understanding legal material "as the role of empirical facts…is itself highly contested."[148] He concludes: "I doubt that these discussions will (or should) soon be conquered by naturalism."[149]

Moreover, conceptual analysis is in all likelihood something which cannot be avoided by the theorist, even on the naturalistic story. Oberdiek and Patterson note that the naturalist must do conceptual spadework in order to go about the task of naturalism in the first place.[150]

Furthermore, results obtained by naturalism in the context of law will not necessarily come to the aid of the legal theorist: they will not necessarily satisfy one of her central concerns, that is, to understand how legal participants understand themselves. Coleman is critical of Leiter on this point.[151] Leiter's argument for moving away from dependence on intuition altogether is something which removes power from the ordinary man in theory construction. This approach sacrifices the hermeneutic importance of legal practice: it entrusts science to discover the nature of constructs which are inherently reason-based. This sacrifice would be understandable where the promise of truth was in our midst; however, Leiter does not succeed in this regard. He sacrifices the richness of description associated with hermeneutic analysis for a scientific project that itself can harbor no claim to truth.

---

147 LEITER, *Naturalizing Jurisprudence, supra*, at 231.

148 BRIAN BIX, *Conceptual Questions and Jurisprudence* 1 LEGAL THEORY 415, 478 (1995).

149 *Id.* at 479.

150 *See generally*, OBERDIEK & PATTERSON, *supra*.

151 COLEMAN, *Methodology, supra*, at 343-351.

C. A Pragmatic Approach

The pragmatic line of thought arises out of the value neutrality debate, as outlined in Part III, and is particularly responsive to the possibility of objective choice as between different conceptualizations of legal material. Epistemic values are adequate tools to make such a choice, and are an important alternative to moral choice. However, though amoral in the strict sense, they do not withstand the foregoing debate about intuitions: there is no method of choosing as between different *epistemic* values except by invoking subjective intuition. They are morally neutral, but are nevertheless unable to discover infallible truths. The pragmatic approach argues that rather than choosing one epistemological picture over another on the grounds that it appears to be more intuitively correct, the epistemological choice *should* be made on moral grounds. The moral input thus becomes a *choice* rather than a requirement of theory construction.

MacCormick proposes that legal theory should be endorsed or otherwise based on its practical influence within the legal system.[152] For him, the moralization of law, according to natural law theory, is dangerous and undemocratic, and a positivist conception of law *ought* therefore to be preferred. MacCormick argues that law can be described in an amoralistic fashion and further, that the choice between the moralistic and amoralistic conceptions should turn on pragmatic concerns. He notes that:

> [A] conception of the nature of the content of law which preserves conscience and autonomy is morally preferable to rivals which allow of a more unrestricted moral range for the content of law…[153]

MacCormick is of the view that a proper concern for legal participants is the restriction of law's moral sphere, and that we should avoid any approach which grants morality a monopoly in theory construction. He is a positivist who embraces formal legality but notes that "the reasons for upholding this thesis include fundamentally a moral principle about sovereignty of conscience."[154]

Murphy takes a similar line. He argues that competing accounts of the legal system should be tested on their pragmatic merits, that is, their beneficial moral and political consequences.[155] We should thus, according to Murphy, employ practical-political argument in making the required selection between

---

152 NEIL MACCORMICK, *A Moralistic Case for A-Moralistic Law?* 20 VAL. UNI. L. REV. 1 (1985).
153 *Id.* at 37-38.
154 *Id.* at 39.
155 LIAM MURPHY, *The Political Question of the Concept of Law*, *in* Jules Coleman eds., HART'S POSTSCRIPT: ESSAYS ON THE POSTSCRIPT TO THE CONCEPT OF LAW, *supra*, at 371.

competing accounts. Murphy argues that Hart's theory is a morally neutral one, but that it is based on a conscious pre-theoretic political choice by Hart to remain morally neutral. He therefore notes that "the very decision not to aim to show law in its best light is one partly made….on explicitly political grounds."[156] After this initial selection, Hart then remains committed to value neutral description. This does not undermine his theory, but it means that in choosing which theory we prefer to adopt, we ought to refer to such background considerations. Rather than making an inference from *ought* to *is*, Murphy is simply of the view that there is serious disagreement as to what *is* and thus we are justified in making our choice based on how the legal system *should* operate. Due to the fact that "[t]he dispute about the concept of law is a political argument for control over a concept that has great ideological significance,"[157] the most valuable method of choosing between theories of law, rather than feigning truth, is to decide which theory is politically the most desirable way to conceive of law's domain.

Jenkins is also of the view that pragmatic concerns should dictate the outcome of an impasse in legal theory.[158] That is, if a choice must be made between concepts, the best way of doing so, according to Jenkins, is to choose the one which will assist our theoretical inquiries, or clarify our moral deliberations. Therefore, if an account clears up confusion then it is more adequate than one which causes confusion. According to Jenkins, theory should not be an ivory tower enterprise but rather should be of some relevance to the real-life practice of law. In a similar way, William James has warned against the possibility of "vicious abstractionism," that is, allowing theory to become so far removed from practice as to become irrelevant.[159] Halpin has made similar comments in this regard.[160] The latter describes theory that is wholly detached from practice as "an intellectual pyramid in the air"[161] and therefore irrelevant to practitioners within the system. The proper role of legal theory is, instead, "to clarify the means by which the law expresses and attains the resolution of controversy."[162] Halpin's proposition thus echoes the desire of those who seek a pragmatic legal theory, rather than the abstract ponderings of those restricted to discussion within the limits of the jurisprudential sphere. For him, the proper concern of legal theory is to inform the practice of law.

---

156 *Id.*

157 *Id.* at 384.

158 MARICARMEN JENKINS, *Can Pragmatism Overcome the Impasse in Contemporary Legal Theory?* 15 CAN. J. L. JURIS. 85 (2002).

159 WILLIAM JAMES, *Abstractionism and 'Relativismus'', in* James eds., PRAGMATISM AND THE MEANING OF TRUTH 301 (1978).

160 ANDREW HALPIN, *Methodology in Jurisprudence: Thirty Years off the Point* 19 CAN. J. L. JURIS. 67 (2006).

161 *Id.* at 67.

162 *Id.* at 91.

Schauer is also a strong proponent of the pragmatic approach to legal theory. He argues that:

> As long as we define all of legal philosophy, or even the 'primary' task of legal philosophy, as giving a philosophical account of the necessary and sufficient conditions for the existence of law in all possible legal systems, then we ignore important philosophical questions while trying to give a philosophical account of a largely sociological phenomenon.[163]

For Schauer, because theories of law have an important practical effect on society,[164] the impact that they have is an important concern for the legal theorist. Therefore, he argues that a morally neutral account of law is ultimately preferable on a pragmatic level: to allow for a situation where law and morality are conjoined is "to run the risk of minimizing the moral space between the products that legality has given us until today and the goals we might wish an ideal legal system to accomplish."[165] Schauer proposes that while snapshot explanations of the law are useful, they should not be regarded as the only option for the legal theorist. Due to the socially constructed nature of law, and due to its ever-fluctuating character, it is also very important, Schauer argues, to make prescriptions for the law, in order to inform its development as a practice. Again, he does not argue that it is impossible to *describe* the legal system, he is simply of the view that normative theory is an equally (if not more) worthy undertaking for current jurisprudence.

Interestingly, Stich also makes a similar point in this regard. He notes that our tradition, which can be traced back to Wittgenstein, rejects the idea that basic intuitive evaluations should themselves be evaluated, that our language games give us no tools with which to evaluate the intuitive judgments. However, Stich argues that it is a "disastrous mistake"[166] to suppose that evaluation comes to an end here, even if it does have to end at some point. He proposes that we evaluate our epistemic values according to non-epistemic values, that is, "[w]e can ask whether the cognitive states and processes endorsed by our notions of epistemic values foster happiness, or power, or accurate prediction, or reproductive success, or truth."[167] Therefore, while the conceptual analyst is content to stop at intuitions in theory building, a more satisfying approach is

163 FREDERICK SCHAUER, *Critical Notice* 24 CAN. J. PHIL. 495, 509 (1994). *See also* SCHAUER, *Postivism as Pariah*, *in* Robert P. George eds., THE AUTONOMY OF LAW: ESSAYS ON LEGAL POSITIVISM (1996); FREDERICK SCHAUER, *Positivism Through Thick and Thin*, *in* Brian Bix eds., ANALYSING LAW, *supra*; FREDERICK SCHAUER, *The Social Construction of the Concept of Law: A Reply to Julie Dickson* 25 OX. J. L. STUDIES 493 (2005).

164 This idea will be discussed in more detail in Section D.

165 FREDERICK SCHAUER, *Postivism as Pariah*, *supra*, at 46.

166 STICH, *supra*, at 107.

167 *Id.* at 108.

to reach beneath this foundation to uncover the basic pragmatic importance of the theory for those who interact with it.

The pragmatic approach would therefore involve citizens in new debate: one which emphasizes the practical effects of theory on society once the theory has been constructed. This is an important question for jurisprudence, and is one which is likely to provoke a more fair and engaged discourse between members of society. Each member would present his own conception of the legal system, as inspired by pragmatic concerns, while admitting the fallibility of his claims, and abandoning the fruitless search for truth. I consider this to be a sound alternative to theories which purport to create fictional accounts of the nature of law. In practice, it will allow more room for engagement and will encourage those who were hitherto inclined to uncritically accept existing theories, to examine their own position in detail, and to contribute to the discussion in a more involved manner.

D. Persisting without the Attribute of Truth

I argue here that legal theory does not have to be abandoned on the basis that it cannot reveal essential and universal characteristics about the law. Instead, I will argue that it is more satisfactory to view law as an ongoing debate, consisting merely of different and competing conceptualizations of legal facts.As long as there's no such thing as truth coming out of current legal theory, we should not continue to fool ourselves into believing that there is. Nazi legal theory is not "good" – but it is no more untrue than liberal legal theory. This form of discussion would allow participants to provide more mature and progressive reasons for accepting one theory over another – not just allowing blind assertions of truth to win them over without a second thought. There are no objectively right or wrong answers, there are merely good and bad outcomes, and it is on this basis alone that we choose. In deciding between such conceptualizations, I will therefore suggest that theorist surrender their tireless search for truth and instead adopt a pragmatic approach, which encourages participants to choose between such conceptualizations based on their overall practical merit for society.

Unfounded claims to truth can have detrimental effects on society at large. Theory has a significant effect on practice over time. Schauer correctly notes that theories "may in the long term influence social understanding of the institution itself."[168] Social perception will affect how the institution sees itself, and thus how it conducts itself, and who chooses to become a member of it, thereby physically changing it over time. Therefore, if the theory's purported truths are unfounded, and nevertheless accepted, the institution will most likely wield unjustified power as a result of its claims.

[168] SCHAUER, *Positivism as Pariah*, *supra*, at 33.

This can be seen pertinently in the case of human rights theory. Human rights are seen as universal possessions, which are not contingent on belonging to a particular state or culture. Rather, they are seen as self-evidently inherent in all of us as a direct result of our very nature as human beings. Self-evidence is not *proven* – it is presumed. However, rights commonly require justification and this justification will generally rest upon an assertion in favour of universal intuitions. However, reliance on universal intuitions is necessarily fallible, if not inevitably flawed, as described above. So, attributing self-evidence to those "facts" requires reliance on intuitions. We might agree that the intuition pointing to self-evidence really exists, and is obvious to all; but there is no reason why rights are automatically justifiably attributed to us for that reason. That is why a pragmatic approach is preferable: the *consequence* of accepting a human rights-orientated philosophy produces more valuable results in the long term. The extreme essentialist terms utilized by human rights discourse gives rise to a theory which has a powerful effect on international societal standards. The results are not necessarily positive: human rights standards have on occasion been used to wage wars, to displace traditional cultural values in foreign societies, and as basic criteria for participation in international relations. Beitz is critical of "the external measures that are intended to induce a government to comply with the doctrine's requirements….in the extreme case, [constituting] a kind of postcolonial imperialism."[169] Without such claims to truth, the theory of human rights may indeed have held less force, but at the very least, levelled engagement with it would have been possible. How and ever, mature engagement as to the actual value of human rights theory is nothing less than taboo in modern international relations, and as such, significantly reduces the possibility of democratic dialogue on the issue. The author agrees with Kennedy, therefore, to the extent that a more pragmatic attitude to human rights should be adopted by legal professionals.[170]

Instead of encouraging absolutist standards, a theory of a social practice should be seen as ongoing dialogue between contestants with different, but equally valid conceptions of the legal system – equally true, but not equally desirable. Ultimately, there is no 'right' way to divide up social reality. Each participant should be encouraged to forward his own conception of the legal system, so that a levelled dialogue can ensue. Each proposition may be equally

169 CHARLES R. BEITZ, *Human Rights as a Common Concern*, *in* Goodin & Pettit eds., CONTEMPORARY POLITICAL PHILOSOPHY 351 (2d ed., 2006).

170 DAVID KENNEDY, *The International Human Rights Movement: Part of the Problem?* 15 HARV. HUM. RIGHTS. J. 101 (2002). Kennedy's hope is that we will "develop a stronger practice of weighing the costs and benefits of their articulation, institutionalization and enforcement" (at 102) and that "[a]s a movement, one can facilitate open engagement about differing pragmatic assessments" (at 103).

fallible,[171] but on a pragmatic basis, dialogue is nevertheless the most fair and democratic means of defining a concept which has such a direct and powerful influence on our day-to-day lives.

Gallie's notion of "essential contestability" is a useful way of describing law in this regard. He admits that "there is to-day a widespread repudiation of the idea of philosophy as a kind of 'engine' of thought, that can be laid on to eliminate conceptual confusions wherever they may arise."[172] Instead, philosophy ought to recognize that there are certain concepts, "the proper use of which inevitably involves endless disputes about their proper uses on the part of their users."[173] Gallie outlines seven attributes of essentially contested concepts, in order that they may be identified by the theorist. They run as follows: (I) the concept must be appraisive in that it signifies or accredits some kind of valued achievement; (II) the concept must be of an internally complex character; (III) an explanation of its worth must make reference to the respective contributions of the rival descriptions: therefore, it must be *initially* variously describable, with no independent method of choosing between the various descriptions; (IV) the concept must be of the kind that admits of considerable modification in the light of changing circumstances, and such modification cannot be prescribed or predicted in advance; (V) each party must have some cognizance of the contested nature of the concept, and be proposing his view aggressively and defensively; (VI) the concept should derivate from an original exemplar whose authority is acknowledged by all contestants; (VII) the continuous competition for acknowledgement as between contestant users of the concept, should enable the original exemplar's authority to be sustained. The final two attributes, although not strictly required for determining the essentially contested nature of a concept, can be utilized to distinguish essential contestability from the radically confused employment of a concept by its users. It should be noted that the seven criteria are not rigid: it may be the case that a certain concept will fit easily into six of them, and may still be considered essentially contestable. They can more adequately be viewed as *guidelines* for the categorization of such concepts. The benefits of categorization on this level are tangible. Gallie notes that:

> One very desirable consequence of the required recognition in any proper instance of essential contestedness might therefore be expected to be a marked raising of the level of quality of arguments in the disputes of the contestant parties.[174]

171 Including my own purported solutions, on this occasion.

172 W.B. GALLIE, *Essentially Contested Concepts* 56 PROCEEDINGS OF THE ARISTOTELIAN SOCIETY 167, 168 (1955-1956).

173 *Id.* at 169.

174 *Id.* at 193.

Waldron has introduced essential contestability into legal theory by examining the use of the term "Rule of Law" on all sides of the debate, recognizing that the same term is used for extremely different purposes.[175] Waldron points out that the rule of law has never been an uncontested term and further highlights how the rule of law can satisfactorily be placed under each of the required headings as proposed by Gallie.

Waldron, as influenced by Gallie, argues that essential contestability is not a sceptical argument about the analytic-synthetic distinction, and that, in fact, essential contestedness "presupposes that analysis can establish certain truths about the concept in question."[176] Characteristics such as normativity and complexity, Waldron suggests, *are* analytic truths which are discoverable by the theorist. However, I am in disagreement with both Gallie and Waldron on this particular point: from the foregoing discussion it is clear that there is no method by which the legal theorist can uncover necessary truths about the nature of law. Even essential contestability, if viewed as describing the *nature* of law in a universal sense, cannot succeed. Nevertheless, I argue that once this part of the argument is abandoned, essential contestability remains a useful way of thinking about discussions which appear to have no clear resolution. Importantly, the admission that a dispute over the concept cannot be resolved by appealing to fundamental terms would certainly increase the quality of argumentation among participants. It would allow contestants to partake in a levelled dialogue, and encourage those who were hitherto uninvolved in the debate to thoughtfully arrive at their own position, allowing for a more democratic discussion on concepts which affect us all in such a fundamental manner. Therefore, each proposed conceptual elucidation should be self-consciously conceived as a personal contribution with an *inevitable* perspective to this ongoing dialogue, which aims at collective self-understanding but might never actually achieve consensus.

Essential contestability thus frames the debate. It allows that theory construction is unavoidably value-laden, but does not lose sight of the practical importance of legal theory for society. Once the dialogue is framed in such a manner, pragmatism may be invoked to decide between the various conceptualizations put forward: since no one theory may be *truer* than another, the most satisfactory judgment will be one based on the theory's likely impact in practice, thereby promoting levelled engagement on issues of fundamental societal importance.

---

175 JEREMY WALDRON, *Is the Rule of Law an Essentially Contested Concept (In Florida)?* 21 L. PHIL. 137 (2002).

176 *Id.* at 152.

VII. CONCLUSION

I have argued that the descriptive debate in jurisprudence is misguided. No longer should we be discussing the possibility of *moral* neutrality in the description of a social practice, since value-complicity in a moral sense is clearly unnecessary. In spite of this, the theorist's embedded moral perspective leaves her with no option but to create a theory of law which is inherently subjective. She therefore cannot claim to harbor universal truths about the nature of law. This fact is compounded by the use of concepts in analytic legal philosophy. Conceptual analysis requires a strong reliance on intuitions, and as I have argued above, such intuitions have no epistemic foundation. They cannot yield objective truths about the world, and furthermore, where the intuition of the theorist is superimposed onto that of her subjects, the issue of cognitive diversity is ignored, thereby rendering the theoretical endeavour even more fallible.

At an intellectual level, claims to universality are unappealing because they are fallible. At a practical level, such claims are undesirable because they are likely to have a more powerful effect on society than arguments which make no such claims. Theories purporting to yield truth will often be uncritically accepted by the majority of society's members and where theories of this sort are internalized within the legal system, they are subject to rampant misuse.

If universal truth is not yet in our midst, all that we can hope for is a legal theory which takes cognizance of all sides of the debate. Therefore, hermeneutics remains an important methodology in that it allows the ordinary man to play a role in both theory construction and theory choice. However, in utilizing the hermeneutic methodology, analytic legal philosophy must sacrifice what seems to be its unceasing mission to explicate the *nature* of law. Rather than embracing fallible claims to essentiality, I have argued instead that we must engage in a dialogue about law which is both honest and progressive on this point. The most appropriate turn for legal theory to take in this context is to view law as an essentially contested concept, with pragmatics playing the role of ultimate arbitrator in theory selection. A more fair and democratic method of dispute resolution, this alternative avoids the lamentable eventuality of false claims to universality being the subject of irremissible abuse.

The Co-existence of Public Positive Law and the Private Normative Order: The Constant Spiral of the Developing Interaction and Mutual Transition between Positive Law and Normative Order

Professor Bidzina Savaneli[a]

"To do just law, makes a dry tree green".
-Shota Rustaveli (XII Century)

I. Plato, Aristotle, Kant and Hegel were preoccupied with the question of not what is the law, but what the law ought to be.

According to Kelsen's Pure Theory of Law, every legal norm is in accord with another 'higher' legal norm that authorizes its creation. The 'higher' legal norm, in turn, is valid only if it has been created in accord with yet another, even 'higher' legal norm that authorizes its enactment. More concretely, the constitution is the basic authorizing norm of the rest of the legal system, and the Basic Norm is the presupposition of the validity of constitution. Furthermore, Kelsen argued that every pair of norms which derive their validity from a single Basic Norm necessarily belongs to the same legal system and, *vice versa*, so that all legal norms of a given legal systems derive their validity from one Basic Norm. It is widely acknowledged that Kelsen erred in these assumptions about the unity of legal systems.

However, the role of the Basic Norm in explaining the normativity of law is crucially important. The presupposition of the Basic Norm as the condition of validity of legal norms marks Kelsen's theory as 'pure', and distinguishes it from other theories in the legal positivist tradition. Kelsen was convinced that any attempt to ground law's normatively - its 'ought' aspect - is doomed to failure if it is only based on facts, whether those facts are natural or social. Once again, to account for an 'ought' conclusion, one needs some 'ought' in the premises. Therefore, Kelsen thought, the normativity of law, as a genuine 'ought', must, ultimately, be presupposed.

---

[a] A summary of my scientific researches on this issue since 1977 follows. See: Positive Law and Normative Order (1977). Normative Order as a self-governing and evolutionary system (1978). Normative Force of Judicial Practice (1979). Positive Law, Normative Order and Judicial Practice (1981). Sense of Law and Law in the Action (1990). Evolutionary Interaction between Positive Law and Normative Order from the Point of View of Comprehension of Sense of Law. Doctoral Dissertation Essays. (1992). "A Structure of Normative order", in the Manual: B. Savaneli, "Modern Theory of Law", ed. Technical University of Georgia, 2004, p. 219-239.

Kelsen's pure theory of law is an attempt to find a middle way between natural law's dogmatism, and positivism's reduction of law to the social sciences. Kelsen does not claim that the presupposition of the basic norm is a necessary feature, or category, of rational cognition. The Basic Norm is an 'ought' presumption and, as such, optional. It is not necessary for anyone to accept the basic norm. The basic norm is necessarily presupposed only by those who accept the 'ought', namely, the normativity, of the law. The validity of a legal system partly, but crucially, depends on its actual practice: A legal order is regarded as valid, if its norms are by and large effective. Furthermore, the actual content of the basic norm depends on its 'effectiveness'. However, actual legal practice is characterized by normative pluralism, and the 'effectiveness' of the legal system depends on the normative order, which is free from subordination to the single legal system.

II. Normative pluralism in each country refers to the co-existence of multiple normative orders parallel with a single legal system such as positive law. In other words, in each country we have a **single** *legal* system (legal monism) and a **plural** *normative* system (normative pluralism).

Normative order and normative pluralism are synonyms. Normative pluralism or normative order is used sometimes to apply to those who advocate plural orders in contrast to state centralism. Positive law is a system of legal rules, which point out how public bodies or private persons of law ought to conduct themselves **ideally** regardless of the functioning of the rules reality. The normative order is a system of established rules, which show how public bodies or private persons act in **reality** regardless of what rules of positive law point to ideally.

The normative order comprises both state and non-state orders. Accordingly, there are two fields in the space of normative order in general: official normative order (hereafter – legal order) and unofficial normative order (hereafter – normative facts). In other words, normative order includes two spaces: 1. normative acts of public bodies, and 2. normative facts of private persons. Normative order or normative pluralism is a coexistence of legal order and normative facts.

The legal order comprises individual decisions of public (official) bodies. Legal order has a **vertical character**. Normative facts comprise individual acts of private (unofficial) persons. Normative acts have **horizontal character**. Both also include cross-sectional fields, which reflect a result of the coexistence and interaction of public law and private law in action, and the feasibility of legal order and normative facts. So, the normative order has legal and non-legal contexts. The notion and functioning of the legal order as well as of the individual decisions of public bodies traditionally have been explored more carefully than the normative order in the non-legal context.

III. The notion of "normative order" in non-legal contexts refers to certain social facts, which have been named by Prof. George Naneishvili as "normative facts":[1] normative facts are the coexistence of different norms in the form of mutual individual rights and obligations within the different every-day social relations of private natural and legal persons' lives.[2] "Autonomous normative facts" in the space of social life[3], nicely catches the imprecision and porosity of the social context of normative order. Naneishvili's position, which is also mine, may be set forth in summary:

1. The normativity of facts does not depend on the positive law or its sources.

2. Normative facts are always prior to positive law.

3. We can always imagine normative facts in a space, which is not subject to the regulation of positive law.

4. Positive law cannot increase or decrease the number of normative facts.

5. The notion of normative facts excludes the idea of the free creation of rules of law. Positive law has an artificial, man-made character.

6. Concerning positive law: Because the specific character of positive law depends on the specific character of external transitional factors we can say that this (but not other) positive laws appeared. Therefore, each instance of positive law is but one of several possible (uninstantiated) positive law alternatives.

7. Concerning normative facts: Because the specific character of normative facts does not depend on the specific character of external transitionally factors, we cannot say that this (but not other) normative facts appeared. Each normative fact is not a possible normative fact, because a normative fact is a fact.

---

1 *George Naneishvili, Positive Law and Normative Facts, ed. Tbilisi State University, Tbilisi, 1930. G. Naneishvili graduated from Freiburg University in 1924. He was an assistant of founder of Psychological theory of Law - Prof. Leon Petrazhitski and follower of Edmund Husserl in Jurisprudence. Prof. George Nanaeishvili is only one scientist who on high creative level develops Reinach's Theory about Social Acts. (See: A. Reinach's major work, "The A Priori Foundations of Civil Law," (trans. John Crosby), Aletheia, 3 (1983).*

2 *B. Savaneli, Interaction between Positive Law and Normative Order, J. "Law", 1997, N3, p. 34.*

3 *G. Naneishvili, op. cit, p. 55.*

8. Normative facts can only be used by positive law for its aims or can institute constraints over the result, which, according to its value, should occur, but positive law can never annul normative facts.

9. In contradiction to the positive law, which always has an authoritative legal source, normative facts have no authoritative source. Therefore we always can say that positive law "happens", but we cannot say this about normative facts.

10. Normative facts should be investigated irrespective of positive law.

Normative facts reflects the normative pluralism in the day to day lives of individuals' and their groups, and, partially by the 'production' of individual legal rules by private persons. The normative lives of private individuals and groups form the independent normative life of society as a whole. The theory of normative facts is based on the idea of contract, treaty, and so on. These include, in particular, private civil contracts, mutual contractual aid, trade and collective commercial agreements as well as the vast range of internal institutional rules, rules of private different units, etc. - but not property rights. Property rights have a static, not a dynamic character. Normative facts have a dynamic and not a static character; they reflect active normative relations between two or more private natural and legal persons.

Developing G. Naneishvili's theory, I underline that mutual rights and obligations of individuals and legal persons are neither psychological entities nor are they mental. The bearers of rights and obligations are related to each other psychologically or mentally but their mutual rights and obligations are related **logically**.

The theory of normative facts moves away from questions about the effect of law[4] toward conceptualizing official and unofficial forms of normative order. "Many normative orders do not have discrete boundaries, they tend to be dynamic rather than static, and relations between them are extremely complex".[5] The positive law and the normative order coexist and interact in complex ways. Sometimes they compete or conflict; sometimes they sustain or reinforce each other through interaction, imposition, imitation and transplantation.[6]

Our position is based on the logical investigations of Edmund Husserl.

---

4 *G. Naneishvili, op. cit, p. 57.*

5 *W. Twining, Globalization and Legal Theory, ed. Butterworths, London, 2000, p. 85.*

6 *B. Savaneli, Interaction between Positive Law and Normative Order from the point of view of comprehension of sense of Law. Doctoral Dissertation Essays. Tbilisi, (1992), p. 25. This work is subsequent development of conception about social facts (Reinach) and normative facts (Naneisshvili).*

Husserl developed a thesis advanced by his teacher Brentano to the effect that all mental acts are intentional, that is, that they are directed towards an object. Husserl maintained that all intentional experiences are in this sense 'objectifying acts'. Husserl's account of meaning builds upon this theory. All uses of language are, he says, referential. Accordingly, Husserl viewed acts such as questions or commands as masked assertions. The command "sit down on the chair" he interpreted as a statement to the effect that "your sitting down on the chair is my current request."

IV. All societies have different normative orders, in which state law does not exist in isolation, and more over is not necessarily the most powerful element thereof. The state has no monopoly of lawful power within a given country, except in criminal law and administrative law, because the normative order does not have discrete boundaries. The normative order is dynamic rather than static, and social relations in each normative order are extremely complex. Moreover, public normative acts and private normative facts coexist and interact in complex ways. Sometimes they compete or conflict, sometimes they sustain or reinforce each other and often they influence each other through interaction, imposition and transplantation. Often such influence is reciprocal.

Permanent and cyclical interaction between public normative acts and private normative facts inside legal orders, and permanent and cyclical inter-transition of positive law and normative order in to create a tendency through which we can comprehend a sense of the law. *The aim and goal of such interaction and transition is to achieve the sustainable development of humankind.*[7]

The above mentioned schema is not unknown to lawyers. All lawyers working in European Union countries or involved with transnational transactions or "alternative dispute resolution" operate in contexts of normative pluralism that typically involve non-state law as well as "official law in action". Concerning International Human Rights Law, particularly law of indigenous peoples, refugee law, law of the displaced persons, lawyers are increasingly involved in complex problems of "inter-legality".[8]

Plural forms of normative facts are based on the idea that there are many real worlds, which are largely independent of the individual's knowledge of a given world. Normative facts are mainly associated with "non-state law". E. Ehrlich, the pioneer of sociology of law, argued that a realistic depiction of the law in action had to account of "the living law" of sub-groups as well as

---

7 *B. Savaneli, op., cit., p.35.*

8 *Boaventura de Santos, Toward a New Common Sense: Law, Science and Politics in Paradigmatic Transition, (1995), p. 114.*

"the official law" of the state. He saw that these could diverge significantly and that sometimes one, sometimes the other would prevail. This was an important step not only in the direction of "realism", but also in deliverance from the idea that the state has a monopoly of law-creation.

These ideas were developed in a number of directions. For example, K. Llewellyn saw clearly that within a major group such as a nation-state, society or tribe, the basic functions of law, such as conflict-prevention and dispute-resolution, could be performed at different levels by a variety of mechanisms beyond rules such as education and social sanction and that different bodies of rules could coexist without necessarily being ranked in a clear hierarchical order.

V. A traditional thesis distinguishes between "Law in the books" and "Law in action".

If the task of legal science is to advance the understanding of law in the modern world, the facts of globalization and interdependence dictate that even the most local phenomenon needs to be viewed in ever-widening contexts, up to and including humankind in general. I agree with scientists in the field of globalization that no one can understand their local law by focusing solely on domestic legislation of single jurisdiction or nation states, that the range of significant actors and processes has been extended, and that the phenomena of normative pluralism is central to understanding law in today's world.

The normative order of each country is a gamma of normative orders of individuals and groups bound by mutual rights and obligations. Developing A. Reinach's and G. Naneishvili's theories, I underline that the bearers of mutual rights and obligations are related to each other psychologically or mentally but mutual rights and obligations are related **logically**. Mutual rights and obligations of individuals and groups are neither psychological entities nor mental. Mutual rights and obligations are exclusively normative entities like norms of positive law. Moreover they are always prior to the positive law.

Different levels of normative order are not neatly nested in hierarchies, nor are they impervious, nor are they static. They interact in complex ways. Moreover, to understand the normative order, the study of norms is almost never enough. One also has to take account of values, facts, meanings, processes, structures, power relations, personnel, and technologies.

The only way to make sense of the overlapping normative orders in the modern world is to take refuge in picturing all states legal systems, international order and other orders in a single monist or pluralist system. Monism and Pluralism are entire process, which establishes a new synthetic system of law building in worldwide scale.

If we compare Positive Laws of different countries inside and/or outside of the contemporary global legal system we will found much more commonality then difference. Principles of Roman Law permeate the global legal system. "Law in the books" has a cosmopolitan character. Differences between Anglo-Saxon and Francophone legal systems are largely superficial and not substantive. For example, the distinction between written and unwritten law is principally superficial, because each composes Norms. "Written law" however is technically precise.

Yet., if we compare legal orders of different countries inside and/or outside of the globalizing ius commune we will found many more differences then commonalities. In other words "law in action" has an ethnocentric character.

VI. I believe that above-mentioned differences should be serve as starting-point for the continuing dialogue among different cultures of West and East (for example, between Christians and Muslims). The constant coexistence of principled positive law and inconstant normative orders is a historical fact. Historically, positive law and normative order never coincided - luckily, because such differences are a precondition of progress and prosperity. But, for sustainable development, it is necessary to create permanent checks and balances between them. If positive law supersedes the normative order, dictatorship results (e.g. the national system). If normative order supersedes positive law, the result is anarchy (e.g., the international system). Positive law, as a monistic phenomenon, consolidates. Yet normative order, as a pluralistic phenomenon, isolates humankind. This is a good balance, like the balance between public law and private law. The goal is to strengthen positive law and to bring normative orders of different cultures closer together, into greater harmony. Looking for isolated differences from the whole is a dangerous mistake.[9] A function of the legislator and of the administration of justice is to create permanent checks and balances between them on both levels.

The "comparative legal families" theory ignores phenomena of normative order as well as different normative orders of and in countries, separating jurisprudence from reality. In this respect, it is necessary to restore a particular jurisprudence, which explores the normative order of each country and then compares the normative orders of different countries.

---

9 *B. Savaneli, Theory of Law, Manual (1993), p. 201-2005.*

Thereto it is methodologically helpful to introduce a new branch of the science of law – **"comparative normative orderings**". Such a point of view is necessary for the strengthening of the European house and the distribution of Democracy in Post-Soviet countries and worldwide. This approach is at the heart of the research on Human Rights and Intercultural Dialogue carried out at the LAJP. However, when and where it is appropriate to draw sharp distinctions between legal and non-legal orders and other phenomena, or between state and non-state law, or between legal orders, systems, traditions and cultures is context-dependent: that is dependent on one's vantage-point, perspectives and goals.[10]

Accordingly, a duty of scientific research is not only to comment on and analyze laws but also to describe and analyze the normative order in its several forms. The plurality of the normative order includes the normative order of countries, regions, cities, villages etc, as well as different macro and micro groups in these spaces. The interaction between positive law and normative orders today needs an adequate conceptual framework and meta-language than can transcend national legal cultures. Such a function could be undertaken by universal human rights and freedoms as a coordinator of peaceful and cyclical inter-transitions of positive law and normative order.

VII. A Hierarchy of norms in the World Legal System has to issue from Universal Human Rights as the peak of the pyramid *(Grundnorm)* of World law and order. Excessive passion for Universalization (excepting Human Rights), is as dangerous as excessive passion with Pluralization (except as the *rule of law state*). The method must be based on an investigation of the correlation among "a pluralist approaches to Law", "an intercultural legal theory" and "an intercultural approach to normative orders".

The pluralist approach also means an investigation of the diversity of normative orders. But that is only the start. The task of such investigation is to discover common and distinctive elements among positive law and the normative order, and then the elaboration of "consensus laws" and ways of rapprochement through "an intercultural approach to law and order" based on the **universal human rights**. The next stage is a theoretical rethinking of the above mentioned "approaches" and the elaboration of recommendations towards their rapprochement. That should be and endless spiralling process of civilization. **Universal Human Rights are the sense and spirit of the Law.**

Summarizing the above mentioned principles I underline the following: Positive law is **what ought to be.**

---

[10] *W. Twining, Globalization and Legal Theory, ed. Butterworths, London, 2000, p.253.*

1. Positive law is an entity of "**ideal**" legal rules, which regulate civil, political, economic, social and cultural relations among persons *in abstracto* through the recognition, separation and/or protection of mutual rights and obligations by the application of judicial force in case of their violation. Public Law and Private Law are the two branches of Positive law. Public Law regulates public relations between public persons. Private Law regulates private relations between private persons. Public Law and Private Law have fields of junction. Positive law includes a cross-sectional field, which reflects a result of some congruence of public law and private law. Positive law has a vertical hierarchy. Legal theory refers to phenomena of positive law In short, Positive Law is "**law in the books**".

2. The normative order is **what it is**. It is the notion of normative order based on the philosophical thesis that there are "multiple realities". The normative order is an entity of "**real**" individual legal acts and normative facts, which regulate civil, political, economic, social and cultural relations among public and/or private persons *in concreto* through the recognition, separation and/or protection of mutual rights and obligations by the application of judicial force in case of their violation. The normative order includes also a cross-sectional field, which reflects the coexistence of the feasibility of legal acts and normative facts. The normative order has a horizontal character.

Legal acts constitute the legal order, which shows the **real** state of public relations in society. The legal order can be directly described, because it has documentary forms, is transparent and easily accessible. The analysis of the legal order is not problematic for legislator. The legal order is an official form of the normative order. Normative facts constitute the non-legal order, which shows the **real** state of private relations in the society. Non-legal order can't be directly described, because it has no documentary forms, is latent and difficult to access. To analyze normative facts is problematic for the legislator: it needs scientific investigation. Normative facts relate to the category of "non-state law". Normative facts are an unofficial form of normative order. The theory of normative facts is an important step not only in the direction of "realism" but also away from the idea that the state has a monopoly of Law-creation.[11] Sociology of Law refers to phenomena of the normative Order. In short, the normative order (normative pluralism) is **"law in action".**

[11] "Normative pluralism is generally marginalized and viewed with skepticism in legal discourse. Perhaps the main reason for this is that over 200 years western legal theory has been dominated by conceptions of law that tend to the monist (one internally coherent legal system), static (the state has monopoly of law within its territory), and positivist (what is not created or recognized as law by the state)". W. Twining, op. cit. p. 232

3. I distinguish positive law on the global and on the local levels.

Positive law on the global level refers to Universal Human Rights Law, Environmental Law, Public International Law, Humanitarian Law, Private International Law, Trade Law, Trans-national Law, Regional Law, Inter-communal Law etc., worldwide. Positive law on the local level refers to the single legal system of each state, which should be compatible with the Universal Human Rights Law, Environmental Law, Public International Law, Humanitarian Law, Private International Law, Trade Law, Trans-national Law, Regional Law, Inter-communal Law etc.

I distinguish normative order on the global level from the local level. Normative order on the global level refers to the state of realization of universal human rights law, environmental law, public international law, humanitarian law, private international law, trade law, trans-national law, regional law, inter-communal law etc, which form legal orders and a large space of normative facts in worldwide. Normative order on the local level refers to the state of realization of Universal Human Rights Law, Environmental Law, Public International Law, Humanitarian Law, Private International Law, Trade Law, Trans-national Law, Regional Law, Inter-communal Law and etc, which form legal orders and a large space of normative facts within each country's boundaries.

4. One of the most fundamental distinctions in legal theory is the interaction and mutual transition between "the theory of positive law" and "the theory of normative order". *The core idea* of the distinction between the theory of positive law and the theory of normative order is simply this: *the theory of positive law seeks to explain what the law* ***is****, in other words,* ***what the law claims****, whereas normative order theory tell us what the positive law* ***ought to be****, in other words,* ***claims what the law should be.***

A bridge between ***what the law claims and what the law should be claim*** is found in seeing the legal order as a part of normative order. Investigation of the legal order in the framework of the normative order gives us an opportunity to assess how positive law (*sollen - ought*) is implemented in practice (*sein - is*). In the process of investigation of the legal order in the framework of normative order, an **idea of law** arises, in other words, claims to what the law should be from the point of view of the Just Law.

5. I suggest a spirally, cyclically and endlessly developing theory of interaction and mutual-transition of Positive Law and Normative Order in global and local levels. Permanent and cyclical interaction between positive law and normative order on the locally, nationally and globally present a trend to comprehend permanently an idea of **Just Law,** which must be

based on Universal Human Rights. The aim and goal of such interaction and transition is to achieve sustainable development of Humankind. Already in the XIIth Century the famous Georgian thinker, **Shota Rustaveli,** one of the founders of Neo-Platonism, proclaimed the idea of just law. As he said: "To do just law, makes a dry tree green".

6. The "legal families" theory of Comparative Law ignores the phenomenon of the normative order, because it does not explore and compare normative orders of different countries, which are in the same "legal family". The suggested theory takes stock of new comparative law scholarship to compare normative orders of different countries *within* each legal "family", whether Germanic, Romanist, Common Law, Islamic, Post-Soviet, Far Eastern legal families and etc. So it is necessary to introduce a new branch of legal science: **Comparative Normative Orders Study**. In this respect it is necessary to give theories of general and particular jurisprudence a broader scope, which will explore not only a positive law but also the normative order of each country.

7. My core argument is that the post-modernity is in crisis. It has exhausted its political potential and is in process of being replaced by a new post-positivist paradigm, which could be built on the emancipatory possibilities of the Rule of Just Law based on the Universal of Human Rights. [12]

Conclusions

1. **Legal Monism** (Public Positive Law) indicates how natural and legal persons ought to act **ideally**.

2. **Normative Pluralism** (Private Normative Order) shows how natural and legal persons act **in reality**.

3. **Legal Monism** (what ought to be) and **Normative Pluralism** (what is) never coincide completely.

4. **The Idea of Just Law** suggest what sort and kind of law legislators (in Roman-Germanic i.e. civilianist legal space) or judges (in Anglo-American, i.e. common law legal space) should make, so that that law would be **just** from the Universal Human Rights point of view.

5. The Mutual-Transition of Legal Monism, Normative Pluralism and Idea

---

[12] *More information: The Universal Human Rights Law As a Pick of the World Law. Religion, Ecology and Justice ... Universal Human Rights Law as "Two Faced Janis" ...www.geocities.com/b.savaneli* - 5k - Cached

of Just Law must be based on **Universal Human Rights Law as Basic Norms**, and this process must be repeated **spirally, cyclically and endlessly** [i.e. dialectically; ed.]. [13]

[13] *Review: "Dear Professor Savaneli! Thank you very much for your summary about "The Theory of Spirally and Endlessly Development of Mutual-Transition of Positive Law and Normative Order. We are glad that there is so active academic researcher on legal theory like you in Georgia! Yours sincerely, Dr. Klaus Zeleny, Hans Kelsen's Institute, Vienna, Austria, Thu, October 8, 2009, 1:56:29 PM 20.02.08".*

Afterword – Dr. Jur. Eric Engle

Duncan Kennedy correctly outlines the post-positivist formation of a globalising ius commune which integrates interpretive methods of conceptual jurisprudence vectored through the constitutionalisation of fundamental human rights as the centrepiece of what I, and others, call the post-Westphalian international system. This rationalisation of the rule of law seeks to attain peace through justice and prosperity. The articles we have looked at here all address facets of this complex process. It may seem strange in this "era of terror" to speak seriously and optimistically of the rule of law and human rights as representing a paradigm shift in international relations. However, global norm convergence resulting from vastly increased economic transactions and instant global communication leading to an ever more intense comparison of different legal systems, rules, and rationales explain why this is the case. Historical perspective is always hardest to maintain. Nonetheless, the principle of global economic integration through the free movement of goods, capital, enterprises and ultimately labour are the clear and continuing trend since fifty years and into the foreseeable future. By correctly seeing the challenge of non-state actors to the international system as a vestige of the Westphalian systems I.R. realist errors as but a nightmarish echo of a soon to be forgotten past, hopefully we will all gain perspective and understanding so that we will build a brighter better world on founded on human rights and economic prosperity rather than military force as the best safeguards of peace. *Fiat justitia.*

Made in the USA
Monee, IL
05 November 2026

67814359R00090